Ireland's Viper

Reba Whitley

ISBN 979-8-88644-323-3 (Paperback)
ISBN 979-8-88644-493-3 (Hardcover)
ISBN 979-8-88644-324-0 (Digital)

Covenant Books
11661 Hwy 707
Murrells Inlet, SC 29576
www.covenantbooks.com

Note from Author

*T*he *Mountain Shack Mystery* and *Ireland's Viper* are fiction. They are written to inspire the believer in God the Father, God the Son, and God the Holy Spirit to keep their faith in the Lord *strong*! Both stories are fiction, but the passages of the Word of God used in the stories are true and can be trusted! Throughout *The Mountain Shack Mystery* and *Ireland's Viper*, Jodi has unshakeable faith, and it is my prayer that her dependence on God will inspire you to completely depend on God's amazing love for you!

(The part of the story where Jodi wanted an elephant as a young girl, the gorilla throwing the orange peel, and the baby praying for Little Joe's horse are all true and actually happened.)

Acknowledgments

To my amazing husband, Mark, thank you for your unconditional love and support. You are a continuous tower of strength in my life!

To my beautiful and creative daughter, Hannah, thank you for the late-night texts of sharing your ideas that are now a big part of Jodi's dream. Neither of us planned on that little random and strange dialogue being used for anything. We thought we were just having fun, sending added pieces of the story to each other. I didn't know, at the time, why I decided to save it…but God knew! God had a plan for it…years later!

A *big* thank you to a very special person for allowing me to share their childhood story that perfectly proves how God wants us to have a childlike faith in him.

1

Johnny sat on the first pew in the castle chapel, watching his grandmother Etta, the only mother he had ever known, get married to the man he had casually called granddad during the summer. He watched his grandmother with pride. She was standing there in her tea-length dress of just the slightest hint of a color the saleslady called dusty rose. His grandmother had asked him to go with her when picking out her dress, but he had no clue why she wanted him to go with her. What did he know about such things? But he was happy to go along if it made her happy. All the things the saleslady said in describing the dress to his grandmother made no sense to Johnny: "Made of corded lace and chiffon, with a coordinating lace overlay jacket." All he was certain of was the color. The saleslady had brought out several dresses of what she called "appropriate" for a mature woman getting married, and the only one he felt suited his grandmother was the soft pink one. The color was barely there, very subtle, but he felt it fit his grandmother's personality perfectly. The tans and grays were not a good match for her at all! Johnny watched his grandmother standing beside Patrick. He couldn't remember seeing her as happy and as beautiful as she was right then.

He looked over each member of the wedding party. Carol was one of his grandmother Etta's best friends and closest neighbor on the mountain. Carol stood beside Etta, holding her bridal bouquet, smiling happily at the proceedings before her. Her best friend was becoming a member of her family. Beside Carol stood her sister Katrina, Jodi's mom. Then there was Coleen, their niece. Etta had become tremendously close to all three of those ladies during the awful event on the mountain. Johnny then glanced over to the men standing beside Patrick. *Granddad Patrick…* that was going to be a whole new experience for Johnny. He had never known what it was like to have a dad or granddad. Oh sure, he had Mr. Ryan, Roman and Reggie's dad, who had been a great influence in his life, but that wasn't the same as having someone he could claim as his very own dad or granddad. Johnny felt proud to have Patrick filling that position in his life. Having a real granddad in his life was pretty exciting to Johnny. Calling someone granddad and actually having him as your legal grandad was going to be so great! Johnny had been asked if he would like to be one of the groomsmen, but he declined. Due mostly because Patrick had three sons that could fill that position far better than he could. Andrew, Seth, and Danny stood beside Patrick. You could see how proud they were to welcome sweet Etta into their family. Patrick's sons loved Etta because she had made their dad very happy. Etta was good for him. She was great for their whole family.

It was a grand ceremony, that was for sure. Simple, yet, very elegant. Johnny's eyes wandered toward the intricately carved walls and ceilings of the great aunt's castle chapel. It was a bit bewildering to Johnny's young mind that the castle was hundreds of years old and remained looking so grand and polished! The ancient castle held onto its beauty with both strength and grace. During the ceremony, the great aunts were busying themselves with the caterers, making sure the last-minute touches were perfect before the last pronouncement of *I Dos* were said. Although neither of the great aunts had ever been married, they did enjoy a party and had hosted many elaborate dinners at the castle for over fifty years. So they were well suited for any occasion that called for one. Etta had no desire to plan or organize the wedding herself. She simply wanted to get married and informed Patrick that whatever he decided would suit her perfectly. So Patrick sent money ahead and asked the great aunts to hire whomever and whatever would be appropriate for a top-notch wedding. The two ladies had been in a flurry of excitement since the money arrived, making sure that the best of everything was there, waiting for this very hour.

*****

With the ceremony concluded, the family gathered in the castle's massive dining hall. Here, the carved walls were filled with ancient oil paintings of ancestors from past generations, as well as paintings from local artists. The fifteen immense chandeliers hanging proudly from the colossal ceilings were glittering like diamonds in settings of twenty-four karat gold. As the family entered the dining hall, and since this was Johnny's first time visiting the castle, Jodi asked him what he thought of it so far. Johnny found it difficult to formulate his thoughts. "It's…well, it's quite stunning really. Astonishing and staggering at the same time! I'm without words adequate to describe what I think." It was difficult to put the castle rooms into words; just to describe how huge the room was would be a challenge. The fireplace alone could hold three grown men, standing straight up, with space to spare!

Patrick smiled and remarked to his new bride, "The castle rooms make our guest list seem inadequate. Almost as though no one was here. I know we wanted it to be small and intimate, family only, but perhaps you would've preferred we had it at a smaller location." Patrick looked at Etta, wondering if he had disappointed her or overwhelmed her with this grand, yet empty, castle. Etta had left all the decisions up to him, and he had delegated that responsibility over to the well-qualified aunts, but now he couldn't help wondering if he had made a mistake.

"Oh, goodness me, no, Patrick!" Etta whispered excitedly. "This has been the most beautiful day of my life!" Etta's eyes glistened with tears of joy and were full of excitement. "I would not change a thing! Honestly! This is the place of dreams. Anyone would be elated to have their wedding here. No one that I know can say they were married in an Irish castle, with an Irish minister, speaking in a heavy Irish accent." Etta quietly chuckled as she admitted, "It makes me feel almost royal."

Etta and Patrick had walked into the dining hall with arms around each other's backs. Etta gave her new groom a tender hug around his waist. Patrick smiled happily as he helped his bride get seated at the long, beautifully arrayed table, where golden candelabras lined the center of the length of the dining hall table, surrounded by floral arrangements that matched the bridal bouquet perfectly—autumn colored roses, fancy daisies, with baby's breath and Swarovski crystals filling in all the spaces. Patrick prayed the blessing over their wedding meal, eagerly ready to enjoy their wedding feast with his family.

Johnny sat at the lower end of the table with Jodi, Roman, and Reggie. They sat there with flushed, rosy faces from the excitement of the array of goodies they were about to partake of. The aromas of roasted meat and the sweet smells of vanilla and meringue from the wedding cake and other desserts were almost more than the kids could stand! Jodi, although a vegetarian, admitted that the aromas from those roasted meats tempted even her! The great aunts decided, since it was only the family invited to the wedding, they would have caterers serve them from a buffet-style menu, rather than one plate fits all. Jodi noticed one of the men servers was acting strange—fumbling about, bumping into the other servers. He seemed to have his mind on something other than serving. Perhaps this was his first time at his job. Either way, he certainly was not a picture of proficiency! He appeared a bit distracted from his duties. His mind was obviously preoccupied with something other than the task at hand. She mentioned her thoughts to Roman, who was sitting next to her at the table.

"Jodi!" Roman scolded, as if correcting a child misbehaving during a church service, "I do believe you dream up problems to solve where there are none! What on earth could the servers be thinking of other than getting our plates of food to the table in a timely manner? That's what our dear great aunts hired them for. That's their *reason* for being here!" Roman said that last sentence with obvious sarcasm and a rolling of his eyes. Then finished with "To quote you, my dear cousin, *doofinhymer!*" Jodi shrugged her shoulders, thinking, *Well, he is acting oddly. One would hope someone as clumsy as he appears to be would not go into the catering business if this was a regular problem for him.* As the odd-behaving man and one of the women servers came around to the kids, both servers were there together, serving all four of them at the same time. One of the other men caterers came, offering to help unload the arms of plates of food and placing them on the table in front of the kids.

For no apparent reason, the lady server cried out loud in pain, "Ow!" then dropped the plate of food she was holding. The food splattered all over Roman's leg and onto the floor around his chair. Everyone ran toward her as she crumpled to the floor. Roman hurriedly wiped the spilled food off his clothes and tried to maneuver out of the way. However, it was difficult, for the woman fell directly behind his chair! Seth was the first to reach her. The man who had been serving the plates with her was panicking and causing a big fuss. This man wasn't having a good day at all. First, he was stumbling about, clumsily bumping into people, and now he was panicking and becoming a hysterical mess, backing away from the fallen lady, acting like someone in shock but saying nothing. Jodi was watching the other man—the man who had been helping them put the plates on the table. He was standing in the way. Seth moved the man aside so he could see what was causing the lady such pain. There on the floor, the pitiful woman was clutching at her ankle, crying and groaning as if in severe pain! No one, except Jodi, seemed to notice how strangely the man caterer, who had helped with the plates, was acting. He watched the scene before him like it was a staged show in his honor! He seemed to even be slightly smiling. Seth moved the lady's hand away from her ankle to see what was wrong. He could hardly believe his eyes. But yes, it was, indeed. He had seen this mark many times while working on their horse farm in Texas. "Madam, you have been bitten by a snake!"

Then turning to the onlookers, he said, "Someone call for an ambulance, *fast!* There are only minutes before it's too late! The area is already turning black and swelling!" The woman, gasping for breath, struggling to speak, said in a voice barely above a whisper, "Why did he do this to me?" She was struggling to breathe. Then she passed out from a lack of oxygen. Seth was the only one close enough to hear what the pitiful lady said, and he assumed she was speaking of the snake.

During the commotion of the paramedics and concerned family, Sean and Coleen got Shadow and Spirit looking for the snake that bit the lady server. Things were so crazy. No one had asked her name or even thought to look it up on the caterer list! There was a real danger in letting a venomous snake roam free in the castle. There were so many hiding places for a snake! How was it even possible for a snake to be in the castle? There aren't snakes even roaming the grounds of Ireland! This was a strange situation. Where did it come from? How did it manage to get inside the castle? Jodi noticed Sean and Coleen walking around and saw Shadow and Spirit had started their *search* behavior, noses to the floor, eyes as alert as star beams, lighting the night sky.

"Coleen, what's going on? What are you looking for? The snake?"

Coleen, bent down, getting closer to Jodi's ear, whispered, "Yes, we're looking for the snake! We must retrieve it before someone else falls victim to its deadly bite! We must find it tonight because Shadow and Spirit and I leave in the morning for their annual training camp, and we'll be gone until the end of the year. Sean went last year, so this year is my turn to go with them. They're getting a bit older, and sometimes, they don't enjoy it as much. In those cases, we bring them back home. But this snake incident has thrown us all for a loop! How could this even be happening?"

Jodi started walking with her and said, "I was there when it happened, and I never saw a snake! It has to be fast as lightning! I thought there were no snakes in Ireland."

"Well, snakes don't get here on their own. There are a few people who have pet snakes, but it isn't legal for them to have venomous snakes. The only place to find those is in the zoo." Jodi had that look in her eyes, the narrowed slants, the perched lips, the look that says, "This is a mystery."

The lady had been rushed to the hospital. There was no way of knowing how serious the bite had been, but since she had such a severe reaction so quickly after being bitten, all assumed the worse for her. Paramedics only said they should know more by morning.

The family sat back down at the table to continue their wedding lunch, which was now dinner. The room was quiet as a church mouse. There was a nervous vibe flowing from everyone there, wondering if the snake, still very much out of sight but definitely not out of mind, would strike again. Seth noticed all the glances to the floor and under the table.

"I really don't feel there will be any more attempts to strike again. I didn't see the snake, but the reaction from the lady, causes me to believe the snake drained all its stored venom into her ankle. An ordinary bite should not have affected her so severely and so quickly! All the snakes I've ever seen rarely drain all their venom. They save some, just in case they need to protect themselves again. It's most probably hiding for its own protection until its body can produce more. This is such a strange way for a snake to behave." There were only two caterers that remained at the castle. Everyone there assumed they were too stunned to leave. They stood by the food and drink tables with a look of shock on their faces. They had to be reminded to keep checking on the guests. Great Aunt Coreen motioned for one of them to refill the glasses at the table. While the glasses were being refilled, Aunt Coreen agreed the events were peculiar.

"The strangest thing about this whole snakebite, there hasn't been a snake around these parts for as long as I've lived here. Hattie and I were born in this very castle. I doubt any of us would have recognized a snakebite. I don't believe any of us has ever seen a snakebite before. Hattie, have you ever seen a snake roaming free around here?"

Hatti, the sweet little lady that she was, smiled with a wink. "No, sister. If I had, you would've been the first to know It because I would have been dancing around in a shocked daze like that man caterer." It was good to have a little lightheartedness and some relief from the scary events, but it was certain that no one there would be sleeping well that night for fear of a repeat performance!

*****

After the dinner, everyone retired to their bedrooms. It had been a long day, and the nervous energy had completely tired everyone. Everyone except Jodi. She longed to spend some alone time with her great aunt Hattie. She loved hearing how they had grown up in the castle. Hattie was in her eighties, and her stories were fascinating to the young girl. To think, growing up and living in a real castle! Jodi tapped lightly on the elderly woman's door so as to not wake her if she had drifted off to sleep. The elderly lady answered the knock in her usual quiet, gentle manner, "Yes?"

"Aunt Hattie, are you too tired to talk with me awhile?"

"Goodness no, Jo-Jo, come on in, sweetie." As Jodi entered her aunt's bedroom, Hattie greeted her with a warm smile. "Tell me all about the great adventure you had on your aunt and uncle's mountain." Hattie knew every detail of the awful can hunt on the mountain. Sean and Coleen shared it all with her and Coreen when they returned home to Ireland, but she thought Jodi might feel the need to discuss it with her. Jodi sat on the floor at her great aunt's feet, propping her arm on the ottoman where Hatti's house shoed feet were resting comfortably.

"Maybe later. That's such an awful thing to talk about or even think about really, especially after this terrible catastrophe, at the dinner table today. If you don't mind, I'd really like to hear more stories about how your family got this castle. Do you feel up to telling me about it?"

Hattie laughed softly as she got up from her rocking chair and went to the bookshelf in the reading nook of her bedroom. Slowly looking over the selected volumes arranged neatly on the shelves, she came to the old photo album where the history of the castle was kept safe. "This is all the memories from mine and your aunt Coreen's childhood. There are pictures of this old place when it was first purchased and pictures where we've updated it throughout the decades since. I haven't shown them to you until now because you were so young it would have bored you. But since you asked, I'm sure you won't be bored now."

Hattie settled into one of the chairs around a little marbled topped tea table and motioned for Jodi to join her. There, in the middle of the table, Hattie laid out the history of that grand old place she and Coreen had called home all their lives. As Jodi carefully flipped through the yellow-aged pages, she wondered, "Aunt Hattie, why would anyone let a place like this go? It's an amazing castle, and the views of the sea are the best anyone could ever hope to lay their eyes on. They are better than all the pictures I've ever seen, and believe me, I've looked at thousands! I love watching the sea."

Hattie sighed happily as she left the table to look out her bedroom's bay window. High up on the fourth floor was a full view of the rolling sea. She had sat there so many times throughout her life. Too many to count. She and her sister, Coreen, had kept their childhood bedrooms because they had loved them so much. Coreen had a beautiful view of the estate's meticulously geometrically designed garden. Visitors of the castle said it rivaled the more famous Castle Gardens in its beauty. The Dannaher Castle Garden wasn't as large as the famous Castle Gardens, but for decades, the visitors at the Dannaher Castle all declared that the garden there was even more beautiful and tranquil than any other. Coreen preferred the peace and quiet of the garden to the boisterous sea. At their ages, Hattie in her eighties and Coreen in her late seventies, the fourth floor was a bit of a challenge, so Sean had a private elevator installed that went up only to their bedroom suites. He knew how much they loved their childhood bedrooms. Both women were appreciative of their nephew's generosity.

Jodi sat silently, waiting for Hattie to tell her why someone would give up the castle. "Well, my great-great-grandfather was the younger brother to the man who owned this grand place, but it wasn't so grand back then. It had been handed down from one generation to the next. You know how stories can build up or lose details through the generations, but from what Coreen and I have been told, the family had all died except for one man. He was like a grandson of my great-great-granddad's brother or something like that. This old castle and land have been in our family in one branch or another for hundreds of years. The generations tend to blur on me these days. Anyway, the man who next inherited the property had a bad gambling addiction and was an alcoholic. That's the reason the property was in such a dire state. He came to my granddad, offering to sell this place because he needed money quickly. Granddad could see that the man was trembling, needing a fix of drink, and tried to offer him help without his having to sell his family inheritance. The man refused, saying the castle and land were too much of a financial burden, then pointing out the fact that the castle was just as much in my granddad's family as his. After all, Granddad was his granddad's younger brother or something to that line of thinking. Anyway, the details of genetics are not important. So Granddad reluctantly went with him to the bank and purchased this magnificent property. It wasn't much to look at back then. It was practically old ruins like a lot of castles here in Ireland today, but the castle sat on over thirteen hundred acres of seascape property. And since it was built in solid stone, bricks, and steel, the remodel would be fairly simple with a good mason and steelworker. Grandad saw the potential, and he felt sympathy for his distant relative. Unfortunately, the man died not long after selling Granddad the property. He left his family in a bad way. Large gambling debt and medical bills. My grandad secretly paid off all the debts so his family never had to know how bad things really were. Granddad was a very generous and organized man. He kept all the records from the purchase and all the bills he had paid, just in case anyone wanted to say the family still owed the debt. We know that part of the story is true because we still have all those documents in a safe deposit box in the bank! The man's wife had already died, but his son and his grandchildren would've had a terrible time paying off those debts. So because of the unwise choices that led to a lot of unfortunate results, our branch of the family calls this beautiful place home. From what I've heard, all the ancestors of the one who sold Granddad the property have passed. We heard there were some distant grandchildren from that ancestor line and that the grandchildren are doing okay now, but not as well as they might have, had their grandfather left them a better start in life. The grandchildren are getting older as well. I haven't seen them. I wouldn't know them if I did. I hope the stories that they're doing well are true. Jo-Jo, always remember that our actions, our choices in life will, in one way or another, affect those around us. Try to be a blessing in the lives of others. Never a burden if it's in your power to do so."

2

The castle had twelve stories in some areas, and Jodi requested to have a room on the top level. Of course, her cousins and Johnny said they wanted to be up that high as well. The only disadvantage to having a room on the top floor was being tired and having to walk up twelve flights of stairs! Jodi thought to herself as she puffed her way up to her room that night, *No need for cardio as long as I'm here!* The aunt's elevator only went to the fourth floor. There were six other elevators placed around the castle, and Jodi decided she would be taking full advantage of those during her stay there!

The twelfth floor was a banquet hall. Two twenty-foot high walls were solid glass—floor to ceiling windows overlooking the sea and garden far below. There were ten bedrooms, each with a private bath fit for royalty, a large conference room, an elegant living room with a grand piano, and an adjoining formal dining room. All masterfully designed to take full advantage of the castle's breathtaking views of the sea and garden. Many kings, queens, and dignitaries from all over the world stayed at the Dannaher Castle and held important dinners on that twelfth floor.

After leaving Hattie's room, Jodi stayed awake, sitting on the window seat, watching the waves from her bedroom window. She thought about the wedding. It was going to be great having a grandmother. She couldn't remember ever having a grandmother before. Her granddad Patrick's wife had died before she was born. Both of her mother's parents had died as well. Patrick was the only grandparent Jodi had. Now that she thought about it, Johnny was her cousin as well, considering her granddad had just become his stepgranddad.

11

Jodi struggled to get sleepy, watching the waves far below her bedroom. She went to lie down in hopes that the sounds of the sea would lure her to sleep. Her mind kept thinking about all the important people who might have slept in the room she now occupied. It was almost morning when Jodi finally drifted off to sleep.

*****

Bam! Bam! Bam! The aggressive bangs on the front doors of the castle were so loud that the kids on the twelfth floor heard them! The castle manager, Mr. Mansfield, went to the door quickly in hopes of avoiding another tirade of assaults on the doors and waking his elderly employers. He had been up since before dawn, getting the morning chores attended to before the great aunts got up. Opening the massive castle doors took a few minutes. Mansfield hoped he could get them open before the caller became more impatient. The doors were thick and heavy. It was surprising that anyone could pound that hard to make such a noise. After opening the door, it was quite obvious why the knocking had been so loud. The man was standing there with a metal pipe in his hand. The metal had been crudely made into a walking stick. Lo and behold, the impatient caller was one of the servers from the day before, the one who had caused such a fuss over the lady that had been bitten. Mansfield looked at the man with apparent surprise, secretly critiquing his disheveled appearance. The man was wearing the same clothes he had worn to cater at the wedding.

"How may I help you, sir?" The man was impatient, demanding to see one of the great aunts. Mansfield, always very protective of the ladies, responded with bold authority, "My ladies had a rigorous day yesterday and are catching up on much-needed rest. I will check to see if Sir. Dannaher has time for your visit. May I ask who's calling, please?"

The man cleared his throat, trying to hide his annoyance. "Waylon Fahy."

Mr. Mansfield stepped back to allow the caller inside. "Please wait here." Mansfield led him to the wide foyer entrance and then left to see if Sean would see the caller. The instant Mansfield was out of sight, the man began walking around, looking into the rooms of the castle. Obviously uncomfortable, he walked around the nearby rooms, knowing he had no right to be looking around there. He casually inspected them as though he was searching for something. He was most interested in the dining hall, where the snakebite incident happened. There it was, right where the other man caterer said it would be, where he had purposely dropped it the day before, hidden behind the fully draped curtains puddling on the floor. Hurriedly putting the small object into his coat pocket, his nervous eyes, scared and staring, took in all the antique furniture and paintings in each room, then quickly jumped back into his assigned place when he heard Sean approaching the foyer. Sean offered to shake the caller's hand and ask Mr. Fahy about the lady who had been sent to the hospital.

"We have plans to visit her this morning. How is she doing?"

The caller shook Sean's hand and started telling him the reason for his visit. "I need your help." Waylon's voice was shaking and a bit apprehensive. "Maribelle was in a coma for a few hours last night. She woke up, but she was still very weak and not out of the woods completely. Her breathing is back to normal, but she still needs a lot of taking care of. We can't afford to keep her in the hospital, and the doctor said she could go home if she had someone to take care of her until she regained her strength. I was wondering if maybe she could stay here to recover, seeing as how this is where she was hurt and all. I have to work and can't take care of her, you see?"

Sean could definitely see. It was crystal clear this man, who Mansfield said was called Waylon, was trying to blame them for Maribelle being bitten by a snake. Sean knew it was a definite possibility they could be blamed, except, so far, no one had been able to find the snake. Is it possible this Waylon fella had brought the snake? That would explain why it couldn't be found. The only proof there had been a snake was the bite wound on Maribelle's ankle. Sean watched Waylon looking around the castle walls and ceilings while he was talking. Such a strange man, with an even more strange request. No...it was more like a subtle demand! Sean watched Waylon, curious to know what this was all about. Waylon was looking at each detail of the rooms in his view as though he was an appraiser looking to purchase. His gaze appeared so serious one would think he was to be quizzed later on the contents.

Sean was apprehensive about agreeing to anything. "I'll need to talk it over with my aunts. Is there a number where I can reach you later today?"

Waylon turned to go as he said, "Call the Cork University Hospital. I'll be there until I hear from you."

Waylon left, and Sean walked to the library with his own thoughts. He knew the aunts would welcome Maribelle without hesitation. His concern was why Waylon had wanted to bring her there. They had only met yesterday, and they had only been there for two or three hours. Didn't he have a family to help take care of Maribelle? What was Waylon and Maribelle's relationship? Sean decided he would find that out before agreeing to anything, plus he needed to talk with Jodi's dad, Andrew, to find out what legal traps they could be stepping into.

*****

The sun was in full array, beaming down warm and promising a glorious autumn day. Patrick and Etta had gotten up before the others and started a breakfast feast as a way of thanking the aunts and family for such an amazing wedding. Sean could smell the bacon from the library. Homemade biscuits were being baked as well. He walked to the kitchen, expecting to see his aunts, hard at work-slaving away at the ovens, and he had a scolding speech ready to land on them. There was plenty of staff to do those things. There was no reason for the aunts to feel a responsibility to cook just because it was family visiting them. His elderly aunts were spunky and energetic for ladies of such an advanced age. Sean and Coleen watched over them cautiously, making sure they didn't overdo things. The aunts had to be reminded to take breaks and rest. Patrick was the first to notice Sean as he entered the kitchen doors.

"Well, Sean, my boy, what are you doing up so early? We heard the pounding on the door, but Mansfield said he would see to it. Did it wake you?"

"Yes, and no. I was awake but hadn't decided to let my body know about it. My brain sometimes wakes before I'm ready to be awake, so I linger in the bed. I did hear the rattling of the door though. What are you two doing down here so early? Making breakfast? You're supposed to be on your honeymoon, you know!"

Patrick smiled as Etta walked over and gave Sean a big hug and a kiss on the forehead. "Goodness child, for old folks like us, every day is a honeymoon. We never have to go to work, so we've decided we wanted to cook breakfast together for the family as a simple thank you for the amazing wedding they gave us before we head back to Texas. Our return home may be sooner than we originally planned. One of the people watching the ranch has become sick. Seth got a call earlier this morning, just before daybreak and came to tell us about it. We'll know more later but decided we should make breakfast now, just in case. We're considering going back with them to help out. That's the reason for making breakfast at this time. Sit down and get ready to eat."

Sean was glad to have a few moments with Patrick. He needed to share what had been dropped in their laps. Patrick sat at the breakfast table, listening to all that had transpired just minutes ago.

"Sean, since I was up at the crack of dawn anyway, I did a bit of snooping this morning. You can find amazing things on the Internet these days. I'm sure you are fully aware of everything I found out but indulge me a bit while I share with you anyway. It's all very interesting to me. One of my favorite things about the zoos here is that the Internet said they have a mirror at the entrance of both zoos, and under the mirrors is a plaque that says, 'The Most Dangerous Animal in the World.' They copied that idea from the 1963 Bronx Zoo exhibit. I find that exceptionally clever! It makes every person look at themselves before entering the zoo. I found out that the two zoos are not regular zoos. They are rescue zoos. They take in animals who have been injured or orphaned by poachers. If they are young enough or if their injuries don't hinder them from being returned to the wild, they have a program that makes that happen. When the animals can no longer survive in the wild, they set up a place for them to live at the zoo. I'm sure you already know all this since you live here, and the zoo is sitting on your estate property. Those zoos are doing a great service for those unfortunate animals! I'm really impressed at all your aunts have accomplished in their lifetimes. It's obvious they have a heart for animals. Not many people would allow two facilities, as large as those, to take up residence on their property free of charge. I'm sure you also know they have background information on all the full-time zoo employees. I didn't think much about it until you said it could possibly be this Waylon fella who brought the snake. Did you know he is a groundskeeper and maintenance man at the Reptile Zoo? He restores all the metal fences and keeps them well maintained. He goes in every day and makes his rounds checking the fences. Then he goes back each night to mend whatever needs mending. He volunteered to help the lady who got bitten with her catering job last night. I kept calling the zoo office until someone was there to answer the phone. The man at the zoo office said Waylon got someone else to cover his shift last night so he could help his sister."

Sean leaned back in his chair (something his great aunts regularly scolded him over). "I wondered what their relationship was. Now I know. His sister…hmm, well, this does thicken the plot somewhat, doesn't it? Yes, I know all about the zoos on our property. They do background checks on all the employees, making sure none of them are poachers or connected to crimes involving wildlife. Poachers are the whole reason those two zoos are even there. Those animals are victims of those evil villains! That's the main reason Coleen and I were eager to help solve the Tennessee crime! We've seen a lot of cruelty to wildlife, and we stop it every chance we get!"

3

W hen the aunts heard of the morning's events, they welcomed Maribelle and agreed to care for her as long as she needed their help. Sean, still more than skeptical, agreed as well. After talking things over with Andrew, they came to realize refusing to help could end up causing more trouble than agreeing.

Patrick and Etta had planned the whole day for sightseeing and shopping in the town of Sea Cove, just down the road from the castle. The people from the horse farm in Texas said it would be a few days before they would know if they had to leave the farm. So Etta and Patrick had a fun day planned. The Reptile Zoo and the large animal zoo were walking distance from the castle. They invited the kids to go along. Patrick mentioned he might go to the Reptile Zoo to take a look-see. Etta knew there was more to the Reptile Zoo than an innocent *look-see*. The curiosities of the former police chief/lawyer-judge would never go away! When a man has spent his entire life, since his high school graduation, in law enforcement, it becomes first nature to question anything and everything that appears odd. Then again, he was right about one thing, the more things they could find to do, the longer everyone would be away from the castle, making it easier for the aunts and Sean to get Maribelle settled into a room to recover in. Since Coleen was going to be away at the training camp with Shadow and Spirit, it may take a bit longer to get Maribelle settled in. Of course, they had plenty of staff who would be able to help do most of the heavy work. However, they did have their other responsibilities to see to. The aunts and Sean would have the biggest part in getting things organized for their new guest. With Maribelle being delivered there today, the less people underfoot, the better. Their plan was to stay out all day, giving them ample time to get her settled in before their group returned.

*****

While out walking and enjoying the many sights Ireland had to offer, Jodi commented on how the skyline and the sea appeared to meet in the distance. There were no trees to speak of, making the sky overwhelmingly vast and open. If one stared into its blueness for very long, dizziness would cause the feeling of falling, especially with the help of the strong sea breeze blowing up against you. It was a beautiful day for a walk into town and for a visit to the zoos. Jodi was thrilled that they were within walking distance from the castle. She fully intended to take advantage of visiting the large rescue zoo during her stay in Ireland. Her one regret in coming to Ireland was having to leave Tena behind. Restriction laws for animals were too much to put Tena through. Tena would have been quarantined and having to stay with strangers. So Jodi was forced to leave her behind during her trip to Ireland. However, she felt certain the separation was more difficult for her than for Tena because Tena was staying with the veterinary nurse from her uncle Carl's clinic, who had helped save Tena's life. The two of them had grown quite close during that ordeal. Jodi knew Tena was safe and happy with that dear lady. But being without her and now realizing that Shadow and Spirit would be gone as well was another reason Jodi was thankful for the zoo being nearby. It kept her mind occupied, giving her less time to miss her Tena and the wolves.

Jodi felt giddy walking toward the zoo. The two zoos had been built side by side. Jodi asked if it would be okay if she visited the large animal zoo while they went to the Reptile Zoo. It wasn't that she didn't enjoy reptiles. It was only that she preferred watching the bigger animals, especially the elephants. They were her favorite. Well, she did enjoy watching the monkeys too. Once when her family visited the zoo at home, they were watching a huge black gorilla. He was eating an orange. Jodi was fascinated by the way the gorilla ate the orange, peeling the orange peel back just like a person would. Jodi was laughing, pointing at him, and mentioning to her parents how human the gorilla looked. As she did that, the gorilla took the empty orange peel and threw it through the bars at her. She had to dodge away to prevent getting hit! That caused everyone to start laughing.

Jodi's mom said, "Well, Jodi, that was very rude of you to point at him and laugh that way."

Jodi agreed but couldn't help thinking, *Sure, it was rude, but should he have known what I was doing? That's one smart gorilla!*

Patrick made it clear he intended to spend most of his time investigating the Reptile Zoo.

"Etta dear, you and the kids explore all you want. If you get ready to shop the curiosity shops down the street, don't wait for me. I'll catch up with you when I finish up here. But if you would prefer me to go shopping with you, we can meet back at these park benches across from the zoos. Does everyone have their cell phones?"

Everyone nodded "yes."

"Okay, have fun."

So Jodi's new grandmother Etta went with her and the boys to the large animal zoo. Most of them were not interested in the Reptile Zoo, but the boys did say if there was time after visiting the large animal zoo, they might enjoy seeing the alligators, crocodiles, and tortoises. There was supposed to be a tortoise there over two hundred years old.

Walking to the large animal zoo, Jodi commented, "When you actually stopped to think about it, how much 'watching' can be done when it comes to reptiles? They rarely move! Even turtles move at a snail's crawling pace. There isn't much to 'watch.' Basically, once you've 'seen,' you 'saw' all there is to 'see.'"

The entrance to the zoo was a huge gate, with two enormous elephants carved from solid marble on each side of the gate, each elephant standing on their hind legs and their trunks linked together over the top of the gate. Off to the side of the gate was the paying booth. The view of the zoo was hidden behind full trees, planted to keep people from loitering around the entrance gates and the surrounding security fence. Just inside the gates, past the paying booth, was a long bench placed outside the elephant habitat. Those amazing giants were walking around, enjoying the windy, crisp weather. Jodi plopped right down on the bench in front of the fence. Etta was amused by her quick decision to sit down.

"Are you tired already, dear? We've only just walked past the entrance gate."

"Oh, mercy me, no. Not at all." Jodi laughed at the thought. "I suppose that did look a bit odd. I just want to sit here and watch the elephants. Y'all go ahead and enjoy the rest of the animals."

Etta smiled. "Okay, dear, if that's what you want. Have fun."

Jodi was content to spend all her time just watching the elephants. Etta and the boys went on to explore the rest of the zoo. Jodi was fascinated watching the baby elephant roughhousing with her mother. The pair was full of energy, and it was great fun to watch. Jodi couldn't help thinking, *No one would ever see this kind of action with snakes and other reptiles.*

One of the zookeepers came to strow new hay around for the group of elephants in that yard. Jodi asked him if the elephants had names.

"Sure, they do." He laughed as he continued in his thick Irish accent, "The baby here is Toby. She's a girl but in genetics only. She's one rough-and-tough gal, always rough-housing around and getting into mischief. I couldn't think of a girl's name that suited her. So Toby it is. She's forever *running* about, rolling under the big ladies here, bringing her toy tires into their food strowed around the ground. She's only two years old and full of energy. Her mom's name is Libby. Her favorite food is bananas. We have thousands brought in every week because all the elephants here love them, even the males over on the other side of the compound. Hey, did you know bananas are not only a fruit, but they're also a berry and an herb? It's really technical, so I won't bore you with all the details, but I found that to be quite interesting. Libby can't get enough of them. The other two over there are Mali and Cuppy. We call the aunt Cuppy because she's forever cupping Toby around her baby neck with her large trunk to correct her. Cuppy's official name was given to her in Africa and was too difficult to pronounce, so when Toby was born and we saw her need to correct the baby so often, we gave her the nickname Cuppy. Mali is Libby's mother, and Cuppy is Libby's aunt, her mother's sister. Cuppy doesn't have tusks like the others. She experienced a tragedy from evil men. That caused her to develop an infection, and she almost died, but she survived and lost her tusks because of the infection. Did you know that elephants' tusks are like teeth, only they continue to grow? It's common for them to weigh one hundred pounds or more. Some, not so long ago, were documented to weigh over two hundred pounds! Wouldn't that be a mouth full to carry around? We don't keep males in this yard. Females spend most of their lives apart from the males. The females stay with family groups led by a matriarch. In this group, that's Mali. Young males usually leave the group when they are between twelve and fifteen years old. The females stay together as long as they live, which can be up to seventy years!"

Jodi sat on the bench, watching little Toby lying beside her mother. She had finally gotten tired after all her frolicking about. She and her mom had found a shade to take a nap under. Toby laid on some of the fresh hay the zookeeper had just brought them. Jodi was thinking about the information the zookeeper had shared with her. Wow, seventy years old. That's a lot like people. She felt sad for Cuppy. The elephant keeper had not shared the details of how the elephant lost her tusks, but she felt certain it had been a traumatic experience for Cuppy! Jodi was curious about the elephants and hoped the zookeeper could give her some answers. "Sir, can you tell me how much the elephants eat and sleep every day?"

The elderly man took a large bandana hanging from his back pocket and wiped the sweat off his face. Leaning on the rake he was using to distribute the hay, he said, "Call me Evan. These are big girls, so they require lots of food. They can consume up to three hundred pounds of food in a day. Kinda hard to believe, even for big girls like this, huh? They eat grasses, small plants, bushes, fruits, twigs, tree bark, and roots. Tree bark is their favorite though. Isn't that weird?" Jodi agreed it was an odd thing to eat as food. Evan didn't wait for her to respond. It seemed to Jodi that he was glad to have someone to talk to. Taking care of animals all day must get lonesome and cause one to crave human conversation. "The tree bark contains calcium and roughage. It helps their digestion. Oddly enough, did you know that elephants can't eat peanuts? Peanuts are too high in protein for them. I'm sure you've seen elephants eating peanuts in cartoons, but in reality, they can't eat them." While he was talking about the peanuts, Evan was shaking his head and raising his arms in an exaggerated question, "Who knew, right?"

"Here's another little tidbit of information, it costs around one hundred thousand dollars a year to feed an elephant! How's that for a grocery bill?" Evan opened his mouth and eyes wide in a comically exaggerated expression. "Now to answer your question on how long do they sleep, in captivity, they sleep around four to six hours a day. They tend to sleep more here than if they were roaming free. Maybe there isn't as much to see or do in captivity. So they sleep more. They are the largest land animals, and did you know that they are among the most exuberantly expressive animals? They can feel love, happiness, anger, grief, and compassion. Inside these huge animals, they feel emotions like we do. Through years of research, scientists have found that elephants are capable of complex thoughts and feelings. I'm sure you've heard the expression 'an elephant never forgets.' Well, that's been proven to be true! They remember people and animals, good or bad, all their life. These girls here will remember me for the rest of their lives. They've been known to revisit old elephant burial grounds to mourn the death of members of their herd for as long as they live." Evan turned his attention back to the elephants. "Well, ladies, that's all for today. I will see you again in the morning." Then turning to Jodi, he said, "And a good day to you, young lady."

Jodi stood up to shake his hand. "My name is Jodi."

Shaking her hand and tipping his hat, Evan smiled. "It's been a pleasure talking with you, Jodi. Come visit these girls again real soon. They love visitors."

Jodi waved goodbye and said, "I've enjoyed talking with you as well. Thanks so much for all the interesting information."

Evan waved goodbye as he left the elephant habitat.

Jodi continued sitting there, watching how the female elephants interacted with one another. They were such wonderful animals. She marveled at how they were capable of experiencing all the emotions that people showed. It was more than obvious that they loved each other by the gentleness the three adults were with baby Toby. Jodi walked over to the metal-framed plaque that had information about Evan and the elephants he cared for. The first thing on the plaque ·was written in bold letters, *WARNING: Do not feed the elephants! They are on a special diet!* Jodi fully understood the importance of that warning since finding out they could not tolerate peanuts and movies show them eating peanuts. The plaque also said that Evan was licensed in elephant husbandry and held multiple degrees as CVA veterinary assistant. Jodi thought about the elderly man she was talking with earlier. Evan was a kind man and didn't put on airs of importance, even though he was highly educated. He took time out of his busy day to talk with a young, fourteen-year-old girl. Jodi was impressed with Evan's humble spirit and personality.

"Father, bless Evan and these beautiful, gentle giants you've created. Give them long, healthy lives…" Jodi continued talking with her Heavenly Father as she sat there, waiting for Etta and her cousins to return.

4

Patrick was having an equally informative time during his visit to the Reptile Zoo. Turns out, Waylon Fahy was a skilled welder, and his job at the Reptile Zoo kept him in the practice of his craft. There were hundreds of metal fencing. Patrick had discovered that Waylon had repaired the fences for both zoos. However, lately, he seemed to have a problem showing up for work. After talking to several of the reptile and groundskeepers, Patrick learned that Waylon had a gambling problem. He was always short on money and frequently tried borrowing from anyone who would lend him money. The crocodile keeper said that Waylon had recently been bragging about a friend who had a new deal he was working on that would bring him a few million dollars. However, no one at the zoo believed him. Waylon was a notorious bragger, and no one ever took him seriously. Patrick was curious to know if Maribelle staying at the castle was part of his new deal.

*****

Etta and the boys had walked around the entire zoo while Jodi spent her time visiting with the elephants. They joined Jodi at the elephant habitat, and Etta sat down on the bench next to her.

"Whew, I know it's autumn, but that much walking makes it feel like the middle of summer." Etta talked in bated breath and fanned her face with a zoo brochure. "Have you been here the whole time?" Etta turned to watch the elephants while she waited for Jodi to answer.

"Yes, I love elephants, and since they were the first animals to see as we entered the zoo, I just stayed to watch them. I've loved elephants since before I started school. Mom got me a new set of encyclopedias when I was starting first grade. I realize that sets of encyclopedias are archaic these days, even when I was beginning first grade, but I have always preferred the actual hard copy of the book rather than the e-book or Internet versions. The smell and feel of the physical book in my hands was something I preferred since I learned to read. The set included a book on exotic animals. There was a picture of a young boy sitting, way up high, on an elephant's neck. I wanted one so badly. I asked Mom if I could have one. Of course, she said no." Jodi softly giggled. "I have just learned how much they eat and can understand why the answer was no!"

Etta and the boys laughed at the thought of having an elephant on their horse ranch in Texas.

Patrick, Etta, and the children met up together at the park bench that sat across from the entrances of both zoos. It had been a great day, and they still had shopping to look forward to. By this time, it was past noon, and the boys were hinting at being on the verge of starvation. Etta had heard a few not-so-subtle comments like, "My stomach is as empty as a football." Patrick decided a little tea house down the block would be perfect for lunch. That would leave them plenty of time for shopping after eating. Etta definitely wanted to have time to go shopping. Patrick had wanted to go to the Reptile Zoo, the kids wanted to go to the large animal zoo, but Etta wanted to shop in the wonderful shops of Sea Cove. She felt certain the quaint little gift shops would be perfect for finding the Christmas gifts she needed to get. Etta preferred getting gifts as early as possible, so when Christmas time rolled around, she could focus on more important things, like family and food. Those were always the most important things to Etta. However, this year had been strange and quite out of the ordinary, to say the least. For one, she was now married, for the first time in forty years, and had the opportunity to visit Ireland for the first time in her life. Secondly, the horrible events on their Tennessee mountain had prevented her from even thinking of Christmas or gifts up to this point. She may be leaving Ireland in a few days and moving to a new state with her new husband. She wanted her Christmas shopping to be done in Ireland. Shopping the Sea Cove Ireland shops was a once-in-a-lifetime treat!

Sitting in the *Tis Tea Time* delicatessen, watching the beautiful sea through the quaint paneled bay window, waiting for the food to arrive, the small group shared all they had seen and learned. Patrick and Etta sipped on their strong Irish coffee while they listened to all the fascinating information Jodi had learned about elephants. The boys were distracted by the rumbling of their stomachs. The smells of the freshly brewed coffees, teas, and food cooking were all they could see or hear. Patrick and Etta ordered simple cucumber tea sandwiches, but the kids ordered the hearty scone burgers. It was the basic American cheeseburger with bacon, put on a scone rather than the regular American bun. The scones were a lot like an American biscuit. Of course, if you ask for a biscuit in England or Ireland, you'll get a cookie. Well, that's what the boys had. Jodi ordered the cucumber tea sandwiches like her grandparents. Patrick and Etta decided to have the buttered scones with fruit jam for dessert, but the kids preferred the delicate petit four cakes.

Etta quietly encouraged Patrick to share some of the news with the kids about why they were staying out so long instead of being at the castle with their family. "Dear, don't you think the kids should be informed about what happened this morning and what they'll find when we get back to the castle?"

"Yes, this is a good time to fill them in. Kids, this morning, there was a visitor very early. It was the man server at our wedding dinner. He came and asked if his sister, Maribelle, could stay at the castle while she recovered from the snakebite. The aunts and Sean agreed that she could stay, and they would take care of her. So she should be there and all set up when we return. It might be in Maribelle's best interest if you kids keep a low profile." Patrick looked at Etta with a grin and wink. The kids were accustomed to his teasing, but some-how, they knew that there was some truth in his teasing this time. The kids thought how odd for a complete stranger to request to stay at the castle and ask the aunts to care for her was an even stranger request.

Johnny swallowed the last bite of his delicious orange petit four then replied, "I heard the knock this morning but then went back to sleep and forgot all about it."

Roman, Reggie, and Jodi all said they had heard the knock as well.

Reggie voiced his confusion, "Why would they ask to stay at the castle? Wouldn't the hospital or family be better?"

They all agreed that would be the best choice. Patrick explained by sharing what Waylon had told Sean about their not being able to afford the hospital and they had no family to speak of. "You can rest assured that Sean and Andrew are looking into this situation thoroughly. After I inform them of a hunch I have, they'll be investigating this *brother and sister* duo with a fine-tooth comb!"

5

The aunts had Sean hire two private nurses to stay with Maribelle so they could take shifts. They wanted them to feel refreshed each time they were on duty and not be overtired while caring for their injured guest. The two nurses, one man, Tom, and one woman, Sue, catered to Maribelle's every need. The aunts felt it was necessary to include a male nurse because Maribelle wasn't strong enough to walk on her own. She needed someone strong to help hold her up while doing her walking exercises. Her ankle was still badly swollen. Sue had the night and evening shifts, and Tom had the early morning throughout the day so he could work with Maribelle in getting her balance and exercises for strength and endurance.

When Patrick, Etta, and the kids returned to the castle, all was quiet inside. Sean and Andrew were sitting in the east parlor, talking over the day's events. Carl, Carol, Seth, Elizabeth, and Kathrine were in the library, and Hattie and Coreen were sitting with their new guest. Maribelle confided in the two elderly ladies about how scary the whole experience was for her and how much she appreciated them allowing her to stay with them and taking the time to sit with her.

Aunt Hattie reached over and gently gave Maribelle's shaking hand a gentle pat. "Hush that, child! Paiste stuif agus neamhni! [Stuff and nonsense!] You're no intrusion at all. We're happy you are well enough to be here with us, aren't we, sister?"

Hattie glanced over to Coreen, who was smiling, and answered with a genuine, "Absolutely! We're only sorry this terrible thing has happened to you. And in our home too!"

Hattie agreed, "We can't understand how something like this could happen, especially in a place like Ireland, but it has, and you are more than welcome to stay and do all your recovering here! Don't you think another thing about that matter."

Coreen tapped her sister on the shoulder, getting her undivided attention. "Sister, you have just broken your own rule!"

Hattie looked confused. "How so, sister?"

Coreen laughed. "You just spoke Gaelic to our guest here, and you firmly forbid the staff and anyone else from speaking any other language but English while our American family is here. Don't you remember? You told the staff it was rude to speak in a language others couldn't understand. It was the same as two people whispering in a group when others were with them."

Hattie sighed with a slight grin. "You're right. I did do that. So sorry. I'll do better, I promise."

Maribelle smiled, appearing to be a bit more at ease than at the beginning of their talk. "Well, you see, it's only that this accident has come at an awfully inconvenient time for me. I was all set to receive my degree from The Ireland Culinary School, and now it will have to be put on hold until I can recover. My health, my endurance of energy are vital to my career in catering or as a private chef. Things look really grim for me right now." Maribelle began to curl and fold her bedsheet cuff again, looking pale and downtrodden. "I'm ever so grateful for you allowing me to stay here. I'm fearful it's a great intrusion for you." Maribelle looked nervous and awkward, fidgeting with the bed covers covering her legs.

Coreen walked over to the side of Maribelle's bed, putting her hand on the sick girl's forehead and cheeks, checking for fever.

"There, there now…everything is going to work out just fine. Now don't you worry about any of those things. You are not an inconvenience. Like we said earlier, we're glad to have you stay with us, and you're going to be cooking up a storm in no time at all. Just you wait and see. Now how would you like to hear me read a little? Would you enjoy that?"

Maribelle smiled a weak smile and nodded her head yes. Coreen had hopes that reading to Maribelle would take her mind off of her troubles and help her to get the rest her body desperately needed. Coreen chose to read scriptures from the Bible for their young guest to hear.

"Nothing calms unsteady nerves like God's Word. Maribelle, would you like for me to read some scriptures from the Bible to you?"

The young lady seemed surprised to be asked that question. She sat quietly for a moment then smiled and said, "Yes, as a matter of fact, I would really enjoy that! Please do if taking the time to do it won't hinder you in any way."

Maribelle didn't know all the details of her being at the castle, but she was certain it had to be an inconvenience for the elderly ladies and their families. Coreen turned her Bible to the first passage of scripture.

"Proverbs 3:7–8, 'Be not wise in thine own eyes: fear the LORD, and depart from evil. It shall be health to thy navel (flesh) and marrow to thy bones.'

"Psalm 107:6, 20, 21, 'Then they cried unto the Lord in their trouble, and he delivered them out of their distress. He sent his word, and healed them, and delivered them from their destruction. Oh that men would praise the LORD for his goodness, and for his wonderful works to the children of men!'

"Jeremiah 17:14, 'Heal me O LORD, and I will be healed; save me and I will be saved, for thou art my praise.'"

Coreen continued to read more passages, making sure to read encouraging verses. They wanted their young friend to feel safe in their home. The aunts wanted Maribelle to relax and, as much as possible, enjoy her recovery time.

"Matthew 17:20, 'For verily I say unto you, if you have faith as a grain of mustard seed, ye shall say unto this mountain, Remove from hence to yonder place; and it shall remove; and nothing shall be impossible unto you.'

"Psalm 103:1–5, 'Bless the Lord, O my soul, and all that is within me, bless his holy name. Bless the Lord, O my soul, and forget not all his benefits: Who forgiveth all thine iniquities; who heals all thy diseases; Who redeemeth thy life from destruction; who crowneth thee with loving kindness and tender mercies; Who satisfieth thy mouth with good things; so that thy youth is renewed like the eagle.'

"Psalm 34:4, 'I sought the Lord and he heard me and delivered me from all my fears.'"

Maribelle was dozing off while Coreen was reading but woke up enough to ask about one of the last verses she had heard. "What is *iniquity?* Is that the same as sin?" Coreen motioned for Hattie to answer Maribelle's question while she drank some water. She had been reading for a while, and her throat was dry. Hattie moved closer to Maribelle's bed.

"You see, Maribelle, several verses in the Bible mention the words sin, iniquity, and transgression, and while they are all sin, they each carry a slightly different meaning and consequence. Sin is a big enough offense all on its own, but when the same sin is repeated, it becomes a transgression. Then if it continues long enough, it eventually becomes an iniquity. Iniquity is when the sin in your life is now a regular practiced habit. Iniquity perverts the flesh to the point that sin becomes a stronghold in your life. It becomes extremely difficult to let go of that sin because you have allowed the devil to have a stronghold in your mind. That's the main reason it is so difficult for a lot of people to ask for forgiveness and ask Christ to be the Lord of their life. That practiced sin has now become a stronghold in their life. It becomes a major struggle to stop it, get rid of it, and remove it completely from their life. Do you understand?"

Maribelle lay on her bed, thinking about all the difficulties her brother and other members of her family had dealt with all their lives. She had heard about God as a young girl in Sunday School. She had gone to church with a friend from school and had accepted Christ as her Savior, but these verses she had just heard were new to her. Her family had not grown up knowing the importance of reading the Bible or going to church.

"Yes, I understand. It explains so much about how my family, for generations, have been unable to stop doing things that end up destroying their lives."

Maribelle drifted off to sleep as she finished the last words. The medication kept her sleeping most of the time, giving her body a better chance of recovering. Hattie and Coreen quietly left her room, wondering what she had meant by saying her family had not been able to stop doing things that ended up destroying their lives, but they would have to wait until another time to find out. Maribelle needed her rest now, and their family was waiting for them.

*****

There were so many things to talk about that night around the family dinner table. After they all had their fill and had caught up on everyone's daily events, they gathered into the front parlor for their devotions.

Hattie got her well-worn Bible down from the shelf and turned to Luke 12:15.

"'And he said unto them, take heed, and beware of covetousness: for a man's life consisteth not in the abundance of the things which he possesseth.

"A lot of times, we as God's children take our eyes off of the spiritual things and focus on the temporal things. Those things are only going to last as long as you are on this earth. Sometimes not even that long. Only the things we do for God will follow us to heaven! People get so hungry for money that they do crazy things. Sometimes, even harmful things to themselves and others. God promises to take care of his children if they will depend on him and have faith that he can and will take care of their needs. There is no need to get so focused on money. Never let the love of money cause you to become dependent upon it and make it your primary focus in life.

"Luke 12:27–28, 'Consider the lilies how they grow: they toil not, they spin not; and yet I say unto you, that Solomon in all his glory was not arrayed like one of these. If then God so clothe the grass, which is today in the field, and tomorrow is cast in the oven; how much more will he clothe you, O ye of little faith?'

"These verses tell us that God is aware of our needs. He will take care of us if we will only trust him and ask him. Solomon was the wisest, richest man to have ever lived. God said the flowers of his creation were dressed better than Solomon could ever hope to be dressed. Brains of transcendent genus and wealth will *never* outshine what God can do for us!

"John 2:1–11 tells us about the first miracle Jesus performed. It was during a wedding. He turned water into wine. 'And the third day there was a wedding in Cana of Galilee; and the mother of Jesus was there: and both Jesus was called and his disciples, to the marriage. And when they wanted wine, the mother of Jesus saith unto him, They have no wine. Jesus saith unto her, Woman, what have I to do with thee? Mine hour has not yet come. His mother saith unto the servants, Whatsoever he saith unto you, do it. And there were set there six waterpots of stone, after the manner of purifying of the Jews, containing two or three firkins apiece. Jesus saith unto them, Fill the waterpots with water. And they filled them to the brim. And he saith unto them, Draw out now and bear unto the governor of the feast. And they bare it. When the ruler of the feast had tasted the water that was made wine, and knew not whence it was: (but the servants which drew the water knew;) the governor of the feast called the bridegroom, and saith unto him, Every man at the beginning doth set forth good wine; and when men have well drunk, then that which is worse: but thou hast kept the good wine until now. This beginning of miracles did Jesus in Cana of Galilee, and manifested forth his glory; and his disciples believed on him.'

"It has been said, during those times, to run out of wine during a wedding ceremony was a major disgrace. You were expected to have more than enough to serve your guests in ample supply. But this was obviously a poor couple who could only afford the cheapest wine and a limited amount of it, so they ran out before the ceremony was over. Jesus was told about their need, and he supplied them with more wine than they needed. Some Bible scholars estimate it to be approximately one hundred sixty to one hundred sixty-five gallons of wine. I can't be certain about that estimated amount of wine, but the Bible dictionary says that a firkin is a unit of measurement roughly equal to a Hebrew bath (another unit of measurement), which is about nine gallons. So six waterpots each held two or three firkins, each between eighteen and twenty gallons. A firkin being nine. The measurements of firkins and *baths* are confusing to us because that isn't our way of measuring things today. However, I think it's safe to say the couple had more than enough for their guests. And let's not forget, it was the best wine anyone had ever tasted! Now that amount of wine wasn't needed for the guests, so commentators of the Bible think that Jesus made that amount for the couple so there would be plenty left for them to sell during the early years of their marriage. Wine was a great marketable product, especially wine of that quality! Never forget that God cares for us and our needs.

"Now let's pray…Father God, in the precious name of Jesus, I ask You to protect my family and me from the sin of covetousness. Help us to realize You are our source. At times it may appear that the ungodly are more successful and wealthy, help us to realize that we never see the full picture of what it took for them to get there. We don't see the heartache, the tears, the sadness, the heavy burden that goes with acquiring wealth the world's way. You, Father God, tell us in Deuteronomy 8:18, 'But thou shalt remember the Lord thy God: for it is he that giveth thee power to get wealth, that he may establish his covenant which he sware unto thy fathers, as it is this day.' We are to remember You because You are the one who gives us the power to get wealth. And unlike the world, who gets its money through stress, in Proverbs 10:22, You promise us that Your blessings make us rich, and You add no sorrow with it. Thank You, Father, for Your blessings on our life. In Jesus' name, amen.

"In this world we live in, there seems to always be people who flourish best when they are causing strife and hardship for others. This is not the way God's people should behave! Beware of people appearing to be something they are not. Sometimes, people use others to gain wealth. Be on guard and trust in the Lord. This seems a strange passage of scripture to read, but I feel in my heart, this is what God wanted us all to hear."

The room was quiet, each with their own thoughts. No one was sure how that verse fit in with all that had happened in the past few days, but somehow, it was what they all needed to hear. Aunt Hattie was so close to her Father. Some in her church considered her a prophetess, a spiritual leader, and a prayer warrior. She was an effective prayer warrior and heard from God on an almost minute basis! So if that's the scripture she chose, they all definitely needed to hear it! Little did they know, it fit their circumstances perfectly, and God was in total control of all the things happening in their lives. He knew what they needed to hear, and his sweet daughter Hattie heard him tell her to read that scripture to the family.

6

Things had settled in, and the family had gotten to know Maribelle and enjoyed her company. She was easy to talk with and shared her dreams of becoming a full-time caterer or private chef. She had been ready to graduate from culinary school when the awful crisis hit her. She was recovering and seemed eager to return to her work. The aunts and other family members encouraged her to relax and enjoy the pampering, telling her it might be a while before she got that kind of care again. Maribelle giggled. "You're right about that."

Everyone had shown concern for her after being bitten and had asked her if she had seen the snake. Like everyone else, Maribelle had been focused on the food and had not seen a thing. She had only felt the worst pain in her life!

During the few days that Maribelle had been recovering at the castle, Sean felt certain she wasn't telling them the whole truth of the situation. What could she be holding back, and why? She didn't appear to be lying, only not fully telling all she knew.

The kids visited with Maribelle often and shared their daily events with her. Maribelle relished hearing all they had to say. Being practically bedfast for so long was very trying for someone as young and usually energetic as she was. Both nurses informed the family that Maribelle was recovering fast. Nurse Tom voiced that he felt certain it was all the stories of the kids' daily outings that had her restless and eager to get moving again. He said that she no longer needed his help getting around and felt his services were not really needed anymore. "Maribelle's ankle looks normal now. There's no swelling at all. Only tenderness when she stays up on it too long. It begins to swell up again when she does that. I think maybe it's time for me to go and allow her more independence. She's been staying awake much longer now, and she's much stronger and has to be made to slow down."

Nurse Sue agreed. "I feel she no longer needs me either. She is making it crystal clear she wishes to do things on her own. She has been taking her medication on her own for a while now. Every time the kids come back from one of their trips and share with her all they experienced that day, the color in her cheeks is quite obvious. She's getting impatient to leave that confining bed."

They both agreed that was the best indication of a full recovery.

*****

Jodi had lots of interesting news to share every day. Her daily visits to the zoo were great fun for the whole family to hear about. Jodi spent the entire day visiting with the elephants. She had spent the day with them for a few weeks, and the elephants now considered her an important part of their small herd. It wasn't permitted to touch the animals at the zoo. Completely against the rules. There had been hopes of returning them to the wild, but these three elephants had been injured while protecting the mother and unborn baby from being captured by poachers. Their injuries were too bad and limited their ability to defend themselves in the wild. The zoo officials felt it would be cruel to separate Toby from her herd. She was not handicapped in any way, but when she became old enough to be on her own, she would be firmly established in the family. She would be staying there with them. When Evan witnessed baby Toby and Jodi's interaction, he felt compelled to allow their friendship to grow, so he never interfered. He went on about his business and pretended not to notice. Evan had noticed Jodi had a way with animals that was special. Jodi's gift was evident, and anyone who witnessed her around animals recognized it as unusual and special. She sat on the bench, backed up to the fence of their habitat, and Toby would reach her trunk through the fence rails and place it over Jodi's shoulders. If Jodi continued reading her book (which she always brought with her) and didn't stroke Toby's trunk, the baby elephant would proceed to gently pull on Jodi's hair then blow it on her cheek and tickle her neck, pestering her until Jodi started to play tug-of-war with her. It wasn't pestering Jodi at all. She would purposely wait to acknowledge the baby elephant just to get her reaction. Jodi put her book down on the bench and started running along the outside of the fence, and Toby happily followed inside the fence. It was great fun for them both and gave both much-needed exercise.

When they tired from running, they sat on the ground and continued to play tug-of-war through the fence until little Toby fell asleep from all the playing. The young elephant fell asleep, holding onto Jodi's hand. She wanted to stay connected to Jodi for as long as she was there with her. It was obvious to Jodi and the elephant keeper, Evan, that they had formed an unbreakable bond that would last as long as Toby was alive, which could cause some issues down the road when Jodi had to return to the States. Elephants can live fifty to eighty years, and that's an awfully long time to miss someone you've become attached to and grown to love. That simple *missing* someone would quickly turn into grieving. Jodi gently placed Toby's trunk inside the fence and then sat back down on the bench. After learning how sensitive elephants were and how fully they related to people around them, Jodi decided to stay at the zoo until Toby woke up so she could see her leave and not wonder what happened to her.

As she sat there, getting ready to open her book, she noticed a man doing repairs on a nearby metal fence. Jodi recognized him as the man who catered at the wedding. She was trying to remember what his connection was to Maribelle.

Oh, yes, that's Maribelle's brother…what was his name? Jodi couldn't remember, but she knew it was the same man. Jodi watched as the man studied the metal fencing. "It's no wonder why he was so clumsy as a caterer. What a vast difference in those two careers."

While Jodi was watching the man, Toby had awakened from her nap. Jodi turned to greet the baby elephant. "That wasn't a very long nap for such a vigorous workout you had." She lowered her voice to a whisper. "I thought he only worked at the Reptile Zoo. I guess he repairs fences here also. I wonder who that other man is he's talking with…I think he was a caterer too." Jodi remembered he was the man who appeared to be grinning at Maribelle as she lay on the floor in pain! Jodi continued pulling and being pulled by the energetic Toby. "Well, little girl, I have to run back home to the castle. I'll see you again tomorrow." Toby pranced and did her *happy dance,* stretching her short, stumpy legs from her catnap. Jodi laughed as she got up and waved goodbye.

*****

Maribelle woke in the middle of the night, an annoying habit that regularly upset her sleeping schedule since being on medication. She just had to get out of that confining bed! Although she was recovering quickly, her lack of strength and endurance kept her in bed much more than she was happy with. The medication the doctor had her taking was causing her sleep pattern to be most irregular. As she lay there in the dark, quiet room, she pondered over the Bible verses she had heard Coreen reading. She had never heard the verses explained the way the aunts had discussed them with her. They were very easy to understand the way she had just heard them. The Dannaher ladies seemed to know quite a lot about the Bible. Maribelle whispered a prayer, "God, I'm sorry for neglecting to read your Word and failing to learn what you expect of me. I've been ignorant and neglectful in my Christian walk with you. I'm beginning to feel like this horrible thing that happened to me has put me in a place where I can learn how to talk to you and find out how to live for you. Before I met these precious people, I had no idea prayer was supposed to be this free and open! The way this family talks to you has surprised me. The way young Jodi talks to you is even more surprising to me. They talk as if you are always right there with them. God, you know how I have been taught that prayer was only for special occasions and for special needs. It wasn't supposed to be done all the time. I remember my dad saying his dad had taught him to never pray so much that it crowded God. Thank you for allowing me to know this family and learn from them how to talk to you and how to pray often. Help me learn and understand all you have to say to me through your Word, and help me make a difference in my brother's life. It's just the two of us left in our family, Lord, and he's in a mess of trouble right now! I have no idea how to make this trouble go away, but I do know that the plan he has cannot continue or succeed! Help me to stop him from ruining his life and the lives of this wonderfully kind family…I know he has a kind heart and doesn't enjoy doing these things. He is in debt and he is being threatened. I don't know why the man is forcing Waylon to interfere with this family's lives. God, give me wisdom and understanding on how to deal with the trouble he is in. Convict his heart and bring him to an understanding of who you are." Maribelle trailed off with her prayer and drifted off to sleep in mid-sentence.

*****

The next morning dawned cool, with frost on the ground. The crispy cold wind sent a chill down the spine of anyone daring to venture out. Jodi loved the winter, and being in Ireland for the month ahead was a real treat for her. It was rare that she got to experience a white Christmas, and this year looked very promising for a beautiful white Christmas. Of course, all the family would not be there for Christmas as they had planned. Seth and Elizabeth had received a call of an emergency at the horse ranch in Texas. The neighbor that had agreed to watch the ranch for them had become ill and had to be hospitalized. A virus had struck their family fast! It was urgent they leave immediately. Grandad Patrick, Etta, and Danny decided to return with their family in case they were needed. Etta promised to leave the amazing Christmas gifts she found in the Ireland shops with the aunts, asking them not to open them until Christmas Eve night.

Danny knew that his dad and Seth could handle the ranch without him, but he had gotten a call the night before from his captain at the police station. Danny didn't want to worry his family by letting them know about the call, so he went along back home under the disguise of another helping hand. Danny was called back to investigate a new development on a criminal he had been watching for over a year. Since, just before the can hunt on the Tennessee mountain, the thief had gone silent. Not a peep from him. Danny was thankful to be asked to help on the mountain crime; otherwise, he would have driven himself crazy waiting for this criminal to show his hand. This person would go into wealthy homes and steal their art from famous artists. He would replace them with a counterfeit and leave no clues to who he was or what he was doing with the stolen paintings. Danny assumed the thief had a buyer waiting for the stolen paintings because they were never seen again. Then he stopped for no apparent reason! The only way his crime was noticed was because an owner of one of the stolen paintings took their painting to be professionally cleaned and reappraised for insurance. It was discovered that the painting they wanted to be appraised was not their original painting! It was found to be a replica. This alerted the whole neighborhood.

All the owners of collectible art pieces had their paintings reappraised, only to find out a few of their most prized paintings were fake! Danny's captain informed him it was crucial he return home immediately! Not only had the art thief returned, but he had broken into a house where the owner was at home. Now the art thief had a murder charge to add to his record. Danny needed to return home immediately! He was relieved to have a reason to return to Texas that didn't require his explaining all the details to his family. He didn't wish to worry them unnecessarily. Danny was still considering the position the governor of Tennessee had offered him as Tennessee's state homicide commander, so he desperately wanted to catch this criminal before he had to make a final decision by the end of the year. Jodi, her parents, her aunt and uncle Carol and Carl, Sean, and the great aunts were all sad to see them leave but understood that sometimes, life throws things our way that needs our immediate attention. Maribelle was a perfect example of that fact.

Johnny was invited to stay with the Ryans if he wanted to. He agreed he wanted to stay. He was enjoying his time in Ireland and didn't know if he would ever get the chance to return.

7

Jodi sprang into action. It was going to be a marvelous day to be at the zoo with Toby. She was grateful the elephant keeper had given her a free pass for the duration of her stay. Her dad heard about the gift Evan gave Jodi and donated a generous gift to the rescue zoos anyway. He knew the expense it took to feed and care for large animals. As a vet, he could fully relate to their medical and food expenses! Jodi planned to stop in and visit with Maribelle before setting out for the zoo. Maribelle was much stronger now, and the family had high hopes that she and her brother could join them for the family Thanksgiving dinner. They didn't know Waylon very well, but they had heard enough from Maribelle to understand that he was her only family, and family should be together during the holidays, even if the holiday wasn't a traditional Irish holiday. The castle's family was celebrating Thanksgiving this year. Maribelle would be a part of it, so naturally, her brother should be invited. The great aunts were in a dither, trying to manage the guest list. They had prescheduled caterers and supplies for the whole family. Now sadly, since the majority of the Texas family had to leave early, it had dropped in numbers dramatically. The aunts had talked privately, commenting on the fact that it was a bit early to be planning another big dinner since the last one (only a few weeks ago), considering they had to deal with the snake fiasco. It may make everyone apprehensive about sitting in the dining room so soon. However, a snake was never found. I suppose that was reassuring in some sense, but then again, not so reassuring. Be that as it may, they were putting on a brave front that all would go well, without a hitch, for their family Thanksgiving dinner.

The dinner was going to be great fun for the aunts because it was an American holiday, and they only got to celebrate it with their American family. They had all the traditional foods, and their American families had some amazing cooks. Since the guest list had become smaller, they decided they were cooking the meal themselves. The caterers could be marked off the list and make it the old-fashion holiday as it should be. After all, part of the fun was getting in the kitchen and cooking together.

*****

Later that night, Jodi was tired but unable to go to sleep. She lay in her bed, high above everyone, she and her cousins, which now included Johnny. Jodi felt comforted in knowing the fellas were on the same floor with her. Jodi couldn't understand how she was feeling. Tired and somewhat uneasy. She left her window slightly open so she could listen to the hypnotic beating of the waves of water splashing violently onto the rocks far below her window. Water had always been a comforting sound for her. Eventually, she drifted off to a fitful sleep that brought on strange dreams and images. Tossing and turning, Jodi found herself watching a young girl in a disturbing and confusingly strange land.

The young girl went to her favorite spot in the woods. She felt the need to get away for a while, but once she reached her favorite spot, she was shocked to find that an enormous tree was there that had not been there the day before. There were no leaves, only long, gnarly branches that reached out far and wide. Some of the branches went high into the sky. Others were low to the ground! The girl walked up to the tree to investigate and felt vibrations under the ground around the base of the tree. She ventured up to the tree anyway, curious about the anomaly. She felt perhaps her mind was playing tricks on her, and the tree was only a figment of her imagination. She slowly reached out her hand to feel the odd-looking bark of the tree. As she touched it, the bark moved like the scales on a moving snake! Startled, she gasped and stepped back, but the tree limbs grabbed her, and before her stunned mind could process what was happening to her, the tree opened up, and she was thrown inside!

The frightened girl lay on the ground where she landed, huddled into a tight ball, too scared to open her eyes. But the strange sounds around her made her too curious to keep her eyes closed for long. As she slowly opened her eyes, she looked in the direction from where she fell, searching for the tree that had grabbed her. The tree was nowhere to be seen! It was as though she had been thrown into another universe! There was a sun and moon in the sky at the same time…the hummingbirds hovering over her head were as big as vultures, and the trees in the strange land were covered with red leaves with white trunks and branches. The sounds of nature were strange and foreign to her, and she had no idea what all the sounds were coming from. She soon realized the vibrations she felt at the base of the tree were coming from the massive swarm of giant hummingbirds overhead. It became obvious to the girl that she was somehow underneath the tree that had grabbed her. The pitifully shaking girl was still extremely confused and couldn't understand where she was or why she was there or how, in fact, she happened to be there! She looked around to gather her bearings and realized there was, what looked to be, a small path going through the strange red and white trees. She finally gathered enough courage to follow it through the woods to see if she could find another person that could explain where she was and how to get back home.

She slowly crept to the entrance of the path and, not seeing anything threatening, went into the thick woods. The longer she followed the trail, the further it seemed to go. She felt uneasy until she noticed strange-glowing eyes watching her from behind the giant trees. Seeing the strange-glowing eyes would have normally caused her to feel even more uneasy, terrified even, but the girl was aware that knowing the eyes were watching her somehow helped her feel safer. The eyes watching her didn't seem to bother her. The girl was confused and couldn't understand her mind's reaction to the glowing eyes following her. So far, the creatures she had seen were as strange as the universe she had landed in. There was a lizard hiding behind a branch on one of the trees. It had horns, and…the girl took a longer look. Yes, it had fur! Surely not. The girl rubbed her eyes. That's not even possible. Yet she couldn't help thinking, what of this so far had been possible?

A little further up the trail, she saw a doglike creature with armored plates covering its body like an armadillo and a rabbit in its mouth that had long, razor-sharp claws on its feet and long canines like a saber-toothed cat! The girl stared at the doglike creature and held her breath. Hoping the rabbit was enough for its appetite, and it would leave her alone! The creature stared back at her, which seemed to be forever…then expanded long black wings and finally flew into the darkness of the trees. She had not noticed the wings because they were hidden under the armor plates. As she continued to walk, she couldn't help thinking she should have reached the end of the path by this time. Before she could fully process that thought, a snake slithered out in front of her. Well, to say slithered isn't exactly accurate. It had hundreds of legs like a centipede, and as she got closer to it, she noticed thin clear, webbed wings coming out of its back. The girl shuttered as if she was cold and wondered if everything in this strange land had wings to fly.

Continuing on down the path, the girl was aware that the sounds of the strange forest were getting louder. All the while, the glowing eyes continued to follow her every move! The girl stood still, wondering what to do next. The sounds of the strange land were getting louder. At this point, the girl panicked and ran down the path as fast as she could go. She could see the end of the path now and ran with gusto, hoping to be rid of the weird and scary forest. She was not going to be allowed to see what was at the end of the path she had been following because right in front of her was a gigantic bat the size of a human. At least five-foot-tall! Wings spread out wider than the path she was on. The massive black wings disappeared into the trees on each side of the pathway! The blackness of the bat seemed to cause the entire forest to grow darker! The young girl shivered and then noticed the eyes that had been following her were glowing even brighter! The darkness of the forest now shimmered in a majestic golden glow! Everything about the large bat was pitch black, even its eyes. The only color visible was its two large fangs, a glittering white that caused glowing reflection in its deep black eyes! The girl stopped and screamed! She turned to run in the opposite direction, then to her horror, she heard something in a low deep voice demanding her to *stop*!

She looked around, hoping to have finally found another person to explain everything to her, but to her utter dismay, no one was there! Only the bat! She looked back toward the enormous bat. Its eyes were watching her carefully. The intense stare made her feel uncomfortable. The girl felt it odd that the bat staring at her should make her feel uncomfortable since everything in the forest had made her feel that way. But somehow, the way the bat was watching her was a different discomfort altogether! Then to her shock, it spoke to her and asked why she was in the forbidden woods. As she tried to explain what had happened, the bat stopped her and accused her of lying.

"I have never heard of the tree you are speaking of, and I have never heard of the place from where you say you came from. I am Absalom. I know everything. It is forbidden for anyone to be in these woods who was not born here. *You* were not born here! You have been fortunate to have not been eaten yet." The tall, grizzly-looking bat glared hungrily at the scared girl standing and shaking before him. With her voice barely a whisper, shaking uncontrollably, the girl asked the bat where she could find another human, to which he looked confused. "I do believe you have asked me something to which I know nothing about. Up to now, I knew everything. What are humans?"

The girl replied, "Someone like me."

The bat laughed a cruel, sinister laugh. "There are no others like you. You are the first *human* I have ever seen! You must not stay here! It isn't safe for you. I'm one of the *meeker* citizens of our woods, and I'm drooling at the thought of having you for lunch! It baffles me as to why I haven't already devoured you, but for some unknown reason, I don't seem able to do it."

The young girl screamed again, turning to run from the horrible bat creature, only to run into a glowing, beautiful dove. It glowed with the light of a thousand fireflies. The dove was majestic in its glowing beauty. Its glow was warm and golden, like the eyes that had continued to follow her. The scared girl looked over to the forest of red trees to see if the glowing eyes were still there. No, they were gone. It became clear that the dove was the one who had been following the girl and watching her. The dove was the only creature of normal size. It flew up to the girl's shoulder and whispered in her ear, "Beware of strangers with evil plans, for evil gain." Then the dove flew away without explaining what it was all about.

The girl was cold and scared. She felt very much alone in this awful place. In the middle of all the confusion, there was a loud, annoying banging. She was so cold she started to shiver. The banging continued. The girl was cold, shivering and becoming more confused and frustrated. What is that noise?

Jodi was awakened by a loud knocking on her bedroom door. Roman again. Why was he forever banging on her door? She ran over to close her bedroom window. No wonder she was freezing. She had fallen asleep with the window open to the sea breeze! The cold reminded her of the strange dream she was having before Roman disturbed her. Her aunt Hattie's devotional came to her mind. How did that tie into her even more strange dream? Jodi went to answer the knocks to see what all the fuss was about, hoping it would be quick so she could write down the details of her dream before it left her memory forever. This was one of the strangest dreams she had ever had, and she wanted to share it with her mother and get a psychologists explanation of it. After all the hullabaloo, Roman was letting her know breakfast was waiting.

8

Jodi's mother had left early to run some errands for the aunts. Since she would be gone a few hours, Jodi decided to write down the details of her dream and then make her visit to the zoo for her time with Toby. It was unusually cold for a fall day, and the elephants were sleeping. They were lying around, very lethargic, napping a lot. Evan told her the elephants had been unusually energetic earlier and had spent hours in the cold morning air running and playing before she had arrived. They had tired themselves out, so Jodi left early. Besides, Waylon and that strange man were at the zoo again, talking secretly and very suspiciously. Jodi had often wondered why the two men were always seen around the same area. There were iron fences all over the zoo, not only in that spot. Of course, Jodi always came to the zoo early. She assumed that area was Waylon's starting point of inspection each day. Then she realized the entrance where she sat with the elephants was the closest fence, and the one guy wasn't in very good shape. Short and stumpy, to put it as kindly as possible. He was ill-tempered, and Jodi thought it was possible Waylon didn't want to put the guy out by insisting they meet in a more private area. Besides, Waylon was hired by the zoo to do a job. It was important to at least appear to be doing his job. The two men met almost daily. The one man had an odd color skin, and his hair was thin and wispy. He seemed to always be angry! He was a very strange man. Waylon was once again the target of his anger, grabbing Waylon by the shoulders and shaking him violently! The man was much shorter than Waylon. The strength the man showed surprised Jodi. He appeared to be out of shape, but his control over Waylon proved he had an excessive brute strength! The man's behavior made Jodi uncomfortable. Being there when the elephants were inside and not there to distract her from seeing the two men arguing caused her to feel uneasy, so she decided to leave early.

Jodi went back to the castle. She spent time in her aunt Hattie and aunt Coreen's sitting room, between their bedrooms, looking through the antique books in their personal library while waiting on her mother. She was unable to get that unsettling dream out of her mind. When Kathrine returned to the castle, she noticed Jodi was quiet and thoughtful after her zoo visit, so her mom asked her if something was troubling her. Jodi was rarely quiet, so Katherine knew something was on her daughter's mind.

"Mom, you're a child psychologist. Do you ever have patients with troubling dreams?"

"Of course, honey, why do you ask? Have you had a disturbing dream?"

"Yes, I have. It was odd and a bit scary." Jodi relayed her dream to her mother in full detail! Katherine sat there in deep thought about what her daughter had shared with her.

"Jodi, that dream is really complicated. It has so many elements to it that I'm certain some of it, if not all of it, has to do with your experience of the crime in Tennessee. I'll try to break it down for you in scientific analogy, but when I'm finished giving you my explanation, I think you should tell this to Aunt Hattie. She is known for her ability to hear from God and interpret dreams. This dream has more to it than meets the scientific point of view." Kathrine sat back in her chair and prepared to explain the dream to her daughter. "It's strange but not totally impossible to see the sun and moon at the same time. It's happened before, but usually, the moon is very dim and not easily seen. However, the sun cannot be visible at night, of course. So we can assume it was daytime during your dream. The trees in your dream represent leaders, people of authority. This could very easily be the mayor of the Tennessee crime because he was never caught or seen. His never being identified could be weighing heavily on your young subconscious since, in your dream, you were in a forest of trees. Now the red color of the trees leaves…red is an indication of force, intense passion, power, and courage. The color red has deep emotional and spiritual connotations. You were extremely passionate about stopping those cruel can hunts. That could be the red color of the leaves. The whitebark of those same trees, well, in our culture, it signifies love, purity, peace, knowledge, and brightness. While white usually has positive connotations, it can sometimes have a negative meaning, as white is a color of mourning in several Eastern cultures. I feel fairly certain that the white bark of the red trees in your dream represents the sorrow you felt about the treatment of those animals. The red trees with white trunks and branches signify the sorrow you felt for those defenseless animals and your determination to help them! The rabbit in the dog creature's mouth symbolizes food. Food usually requires chewing. Do you remember the old saying, *I need to chew on that for a while*? That, again, could be referring to the mayor. Your brain feels the need to think about him enough to find out who he is.

"Giant hummingbirds and other flying creatures is a sign that all that has happened to you is bigger than your young mind can handle on your own. That's probably the reason all the creatures in the forest had wings to fly. Your subconscious is trying to rise above your problems. Hummingbirds also invite you to look at the bigger picture and see the divine connection in everything you have experienced. That's another reason I think Aunt Hattie needs to hear your dream. The large fangs and teeth you saw go along with the need to think things through [the need to chew on things for a while]. Dogs in dreams can mean close friends or a deceiver. Since this dog was covered in armor and it had the rabbit [food] in its mouth [the need to think things through], I'd say it isn't a friend being represented here. The tree that grabbed you at the beginning of the dream is a hijacker. Usually, an enemy is trying to take control of your life. Bats are nocturnal animals and mostly stir around during the night. Since we've established that your dream must be during the day and the bat said he wanted to eat you for his lunch, we are to assume that the bat is to be associated with death and darkness. This could also be from the horrible Tennessee crime you experienced. The snake you saw, they usually mean lies. Remember the snake in the Garden of Eden?

However, in your dream, the snake had legs like a centipede. That usually means you are letting your fears get the best of you. Your fears may be running your life out of control, stopping you from progressing in your life, hindering you from thinking clearly. As long as you dwell on things you can't control, you are not living your life based on faith. You may even feel you are being shut out of important decisions. This can cause you to feel desperate to make unwise choices. This dream could be a way of making you aware that you need to rely on God and stop dwelling on things too big for you. Jodi, this all ties in with your experience during the crime in Tennessee. The bat told you that no one was allowed in the forest that wasn't born there. Well, that's the same law of Bear Mountain. The chief has a law of the mountain. You must be born there or approved by the committee to live there. You knew those evil men had no right to be on the mountain. This dream of yours is your subconscious mind dealing with the stress you have been feeling this past summer. It was too awful for your young brain to understand, and the stress of it is showing up in your dreams. However, this dream feels to me to be more than mere stress. Let's go have a long talk with Aunt Hattie."

Jodi and her mother left to look for the sweet, gentle aunt. Hattie was known for her relationship with her Heavenly Father. Many considered Aunt Hattie to be like a modern-day Deborah of Judges 4 and 5. She was Baptist. She had belonged to the Baptist church since she had accepted Christ into her life, and the pastor of the castle's chapel was a Baptist preacher; however, Hattie never was one who set big expectations on the denomination alone. Her only belief was God and His Word. The church where Hattie grew up felt that, even as a child, she went a bit overboard with her believing and talking to God. They attributed it to her being young and her not being mature enough to have a grasp on reality. Hattie's parents were thankful she was young enough to have full faith in God, and they encouraged her to build on that faith! Now that Hattie was older, she understood other people's reluctance. For the most part, the people she had grown up around were quiet, conservative Baptists. There wasn't a lot of shouting or showing of emotions in the church or elsewhere. Hattie was that way too, but only to a certain degree. If she felt the Lord leading her to say something or pray for someone, dear Hattie did it! And she did it without explanation or apology! There were many in her church that didn't feel comfortable with that. Oddly enough, the people to whom she felt led to talk to or pray for were never the ones speaking against her doing it. It was always the ones observing what she did that had the complaints. Since Hattie and Coreen had felt led to open up a chapel at the castle, they had regular opportunities to minister to people all over the world. The Dannaher Castle was the only bed and breakfast in all of Ireland that had a pastor on staff for all the guests who may need spiritual counseling. Jodi and her mother found Hattie in the castle's formal library, reading her well-worn Bible. Hattie had several times each day where she would spend time with her Bible and talking to God. Of course, Aunt Hattie was a lot like Jodi in the way she talked with God. She talked with her Heavenly Father all the time. She never needed to be having a devotional or special time for prayer. Hattie talked to God all the time.

Jodi and her mother walked in quietly. Then Kathrine cleared her throat and said, "Ahem, Aunt Hattie, we hate to disturb your quiet time, but we have a bit of a dilemma. We need your insight. Could you spare a few minutes, please?"

The elderly aunt removed her metal-framed reading glasses with a huge smile. "Of course. Come have a seat. You're not disturbing me at all." Jodi sat down in the chair next to her aunt and shared her dream and her mom's scientific interpretation with her. After Jodi had finished telling her dream, the three of them sat there in silence for a good long while. Hattie sat looking at Jodi with an intensity that made the young girl a little shy and awkward. "Give me just a minute, my dear. I need to listen to what our Father has to say about this dream of yours. His explanation will clear this up for you."

Then the godly lady leaned back into her rocking chair and closed her eyes. There was a long pause. Jodi watched as her great aunt leaned back comfortably in her rocking chair, continuing to rock slowly, back and forth as if she had drifted off for a quick nap. But that wasn't likely, because she was still rocking slowly. Still remaining silent, Jodi looked over to her mother, wondering if their aunt had accidentally fallen asleep. They continued sitting there, unsure of what to do. There was a chill in the air, and there was a fire going in the fireplace. Jodi was reminded, once again, how loud a burning fire could be. After a few minutes, which seemed to Jodi to be an hour, Aunt Hattie sat up straight in her chair, took Jodi by both her hands, and became solemnly serious.

"My dear, sweet child, everything your mom said about this dream is true. Our brains are an amazing gift from God. Sometimes, the stresses of our days do show up in our dreams. More often than not, they are weird and strange. Lots of times, they make no sense at all! These strange dreams are our brains' way of dealing with the stress and helping our minds to work out and relieve some of the collected stress. That's what is going on in your young brain, but there is another reason God is allowing this particular dream. I may repeat myself, but it's because it is important that you remember all that is being said. Not only did it help work out stress from your brain, but it is also a message from God. Now here is the spiritual interpretation of that same dream. This dream is a warning to you. We all know that children are to be wary of strangers, but for some reason, God felt it necessary to forewarn you in a dream to be aware of a stranger. We all know this is a good practice to follow; however, this is a specific warning! The trees represent an adult with authority. Since there is more than one tree, a forest of trees, we can assume that the person of authority is one with powerful influence. It could possibly be the mayor guy everyone was wondering about. You have been thinking about him often, so he's most probably the reason for the trees in your dream.

"The psychological meaning behind the dog is to think about the things that have happened to you [chew on things]. However, the rabbit in your dream represents *strong meat, strong spiritually*. The rabbit had strong claws and long, strong saber teeth. That tells me it was a strong animal to capture. Pay close attention to the reason the strong rabbit ended up in the dog creature's mouth! The dog creature was cunning. It had to catch the strong rabbit off guard before it could be captured. You, dear Jodi, need to stay alert spiritually and physically! You need to think about the things you have experienced but think about them through the eyes of your strong faith. Not naturally. You, my dear Jodi, are unusually strong in your faith in God, especially for someone so young. You have a reputation for talking to God on a regular, even random basis, and that, my dear girl, is proof that your faith in God is unusually strong for one your age! That kind of faith is unwavering and may be in for great testing. God is preparing you for that test! Only the mature Christian can understand the deep teachings of God's Word. Hebrews 5:14 tells us, 'But strong meat belongeth to those who by reason of use have their senses exercised and recognize the evil that may come your way.'

"In your dream, the dog creature was holding a large rabbit with saber-tooth fangs and large claws. That represents strong *meat*. Jodi, this is just reminding you that you are strong spiritually, and your faith in God is remarkable! God is letting you know that your faith may be tested, so hold strong like you always do! The strong rabbit was captured because it was caught off guard, but you won't be caught off guard if you keep your faith strong! The eyes you saw following and watching you through the trees are letting you know that God sees everything and is always with you. In your dream, they seemed mysterious to you. That's because the guidance and watch care of the Holy Spirit is mysterious to us. His ability to help us depends totally on our ability to have faith. Anyone who is not a believer cannot understand how the Holy Spirit works in the lives of believers. Keep the faith in God's ability to guide you in whatever may come your way. The large black bat in your dream is the evil that wishes to devour you, but even he admitted that he couldn't do that! God is telling you not to be fearful because you are protected.

"Remember the Scripture Psalm 118:6, 'The LORD is on my side; I will not fear: what can man do to me?' The bat also told you his name, Absalom. The Hebrew meaning of that name is Father of Peace. Handsome prince. However, remember the character of David's son, Absalom. He was a traitor and wanted to kill his father, a very deceptive character, and the bat in your dream represents someone who will try to harm you. Maybe someone you have seen and find strange. Stay alert to anyone you don't know. He or she could be the one with evil motives. That is what the bat is representing in your dream! The bat informed you that you were not allowed in the forbidden woods. Only the ones born there were allowed there. Jodi, the forbidden woods represent worry, doubt, and fear! That was a way of informing you that worry and fear are not allowed in a Christian's life. As God's children, faith is the only way we are to think and feel. Worry, doubt, and fear are all intruders in the hearts and minds of believers. Those feelings don't belong there and should only be found in the minds of those who don't have God in their lives to turn to. The devil will cause everyone he can to experience those feelings, but a child of God has the Holy Spirit to fight those feelings off. The dove you saw in your dream, I saw more detail to the dove than you mentioned. You may have forgotten, or it may not have seemed important because of all the other overwhelming sights you saw. The dove I saw had a distinctive nose, muscular thighs, and long toes. Do you remember those in your dream?"

Jodi sat there, pondering in her mind what the dove had actually looked like. "Yes, they were *very* distinctive! I overlooked them because the girl had turned to run away from that horrid bat! I had only a quick glimpse of the dove because it flew to the girl's shoulder and began whispering in her ear! I never gave its appearance another thought." Jodi was shocked that her aunt had seen the same dove that she had seen in her dream!

"God is so amazing!" Her great aunt smiled. "That's perfectly natural, my dear. God brought it to my attention so I could tell you the reason for the dove's appearance in your dream. The nose is for discernment. You have a keen gift of discernment, especially for one as young as you are. However, be alert to your surroundings more than usual. The thighs are strong. One of the strongest muscles in the body. In your dream, they represent faith. Keep your faith strong! Keep trusting that God is in control. You may have a scary encounter, but there's no need for you to be afraid. The toes are balanced. Keep a level head if something doesn't feel right. Be on guard! Don't let the situation, no matter how confusing or scary, cause you to lose your head and panic. If something odd should happen and you feel afraid, take a second and allow your mind to remember your dream. Allow the Holy Spirit to calm you and work through you.

Remember, God is showing you this dream so that you will know before it happens that you will be taken care of. God himself is going to take care of you! Jo-Jo, this dream of yours is a warning to stay alert. It's a reminder that you have gone through the stress that your young mind is struggling to deal with. It's possible you may have more to deal with. Just pray and be alert to your surroundings. This dream is a reminder that you are close to God and to let you know he is close to you. You know His Word, so continue to trust Him. Something may be going to happen in your near future. God wants you to be forewarned so it will be easier to trust him if something happens. Just like the dove was keeping an eye on the girl in your dream, the Holy Spirit is with you all the time! Now let me pray for you...

"My Father God, You are Jodi's refuge and her fortress, her God, in You will she trust. Surely, You will deliver her from the fowler [from the crafty hunter] and from the noisome pestilence [any evil that wishes to harm her]. You shall cover her with Your feathers, and under Your wings, she will trust. Your truth will be her shield and buckler. Give her peace of mind and the understanding that You have her covered and protected! Thank You for preparing her for the testing of her faith. Father, in Matthew 16:19, You tell us that You gave us the keys to the kingdom of heaven, and whatsoever we bind on earth will be bound in heaven, and whatsoever we lose on earth will be loosed in heaven...Father, in the name of Jesus, we bind the efforts of this enemy You have warned Jodi about! We lose the angels You tell us about in Psalm 91. Guard Jodi with Your mighty hand! In Job 22:28, You tell us, we will declare a thing, and it shall be established for us, and light will shine on our ways. Father, I am declaring not only will Jodi be protected, but she will also stand strong! She will be bold in her confidence in the Holy Spirit to guide her. Father, we are depending on You to shine light on the situation You are warning Jodi about and that You will give her courage and great victory over the evil! In Jesus' name, amen.

"Now, Jodi, I want you to take these scriptures and meditate on them during your devotionals. This is vitally important!

"Ephesians 6:11–13, 'Put on the whole armor of God, that ye may be able to stand against the wiles of the devil. For we wrestle not against flesh and blood, but against principalities, against powers, against the rulers of darkness in high places. Wherefore take unto you the whole armor of God, that ye may be able to withstand in the evil day, and having done all, to stand.'

"II Corinthians 10:4–5, 'For the weapons of our warfare are not carnal, but mighty through God to the pulling down of strongholds; Casting down imaginations, and every high thing that exalteth itself against the knowledge of God, and bringing into captivity every thought to the obedience of Christ.'

"Now, my dear great-niece, this next verse is for your courage.

"Luke 10:19, 'Behold, I give unto you power to tread on serpents and scorpions, and overall power of the enemy: and nothing shall by any means hurt you.'

"Go in peace, my dear child. You will conquer this enemy like you have conquered all the others you have encountered in your young Christian life!"

9

With all the new developments going on with Maribelle's recovery, family members having to leave early, and Jodi's strange warning in a dream, Thanksgiving had sneaked up on them almost without their being prepared. The aunts were thankful for the castle staff because they had kept the necessary plans going for their Thanksgiving to go smoothly. All the ladies were in the kitchen, cooking up a storm, chatting merrily over all the delicious goodies being prepared. Before having to go back to Texas, Danny had gone hunting with Sean and had gotten a fat turkey for the meal. Patrick had agreed to dress it but insisted the boys help with the task. He felt it was important for them to learn the basic skills of preserving the food. The day Kathrine had taken the trip to town to run the errands for the aunts, she had purchased Jodi some of the vegan meats for her meal. It wasn't that Jodi never ate meat. Occasionally, she ate a small amount when visiting with friends or family members who didn't have anything else, because she was sensitive to others' feelings and would never want to hurt or embarrass anyone, but she preferred not to eat animals. Most often, there were plenty of other things to enjoy without the meat. This meal would be no exception. The castle's huge dining buffet was loaded with delicious goodies for everyone. The twenty-two-pound turkey, all roasted brown and juicy, waiting to be carved, mound upon mounds of dressing, potato salad, huge vats of baked beans, slaw, stuffed eggs, homemade cranberry sauce, yeast rolls, and the dessert table was just as heavy with sweet confections—pumpkin pie, pecan pie, sweet potato casserole, and carrot cake. It was a feast the aunts only experienced when their American family came for the holidays. Amazing Southern food that they fully intended to relish!

Maribelle was having the best time of her life, helping the ladies prepare the feast. It was her first time in a very long time being included in a family holiday meal and being able to get out of her sickbed made it even better. The turkey and dressing were a first for her. She enjoyed learning new dishes to add to her growing food register. The aunts watched her carefully, making sure she didn't over-exert herself and noticed her expert ability to handle and prepare food. They were quite impressed. The family noticed that Waylon didn't come but chose not to mention it. Maribelle seemed very private where her brother was concerned, and no one wished to cause her any additional stress by pressing the issue. Maribelle knew her brother had been invited and was welcome to join them. That was all that was important.

The family all gathered in the dining room, once again, for a feast of Thanksgiving. Being in the dining room for the first time since the accident was a bit strange, but no one let on about it. The meals, up to this point, had been eaten in the kitchen at the large breakfast table. There was plenty of room there, and the space felt much cozier than the large formal dining room. However, the day to celebrate Thanksgiving needed to be special and grand. Without Granddad Patrick there, Aunt Hattie felt Uncle Carl should pray the blessing over the Thanksgiving meal. He was, after all, the next elder gentleman in the family. Carl bowed his head, and the rest of the family did the same.

"Father God, we are so thankful for the blessings You have given us every day of our lives. You show us daily how much You love us. Please forgive our lack of trust when we doubt and our lack of appreciation when we complain. We are looking to You to show us how to properly and totally worship You. We desire to be obedient to Your will and become all that You created us to be. Thank You for this amazing meal, and thank You for the freedom in the United States of America. In Jesus' name, amen."

*****

Thanksgiving was over, and the weather had become cold and felt like winter. Back in the States, in the South, things would still feel like summer. This was a new experience for the American family, and the kids thoroughly enjoyed it. The trips to the zoo were a bit uncomfortable for the outdoors, so Evan, understanding the visits were important to the elephants, set up an inside space for Jodi to come to each day. There was a happy feel to the elephants when Jodi came by. Evan noticed the difference every time she came for a visit. Those elephants loved Jodi. She loved them as well and often dreaded the time when she would no longer be close to see them every day. Well, the weekends were good practice for that because the zoo was closed on Sundays, and that was great practice for both Jodi and the elephants to have time apart.

Sundays were a bit different at the castle because they didn't need to leave to go to church. The chapel was inside the castle, and they had their own pastor who preached every Sunday for the services. The visiting family always enjoyed going to church, and they enjoyed this new experience quite a bit. They all looked forward to the weekly sermons.

Pastor John was in rare form this Sunday and eager to get started. "God tells us He knew us before we were born. Stop and think about that for a moment. God knew us before we were born. That can only mean one of two things. One, we were already an existing spirit, waiting to be born, or two, we were real in God's mind. Just like the earth before it was created, it already existed in God's mind. He already knew it all! He knew us in his mind before he brought us into human form! Either way, if you were ever conceived, ready to be born, it is because God wanted you to exist. Therefore, He had a plan for everyone He placed in the womb! He had a plan for our lives when He created us.

"Jeremiah 1:5, 'Before I formed thee in the belly, I knew thee; and before thou comest forth out of the womb, I sanctified thee, and I ordained thee a prophet unto the nations.' Jeremiah was a priest ordained by the Lord. He had a lot of difficult times in his life. He witnessed his country being destroyed and his people being taken into captivity. He was very young to have experienced all this hardship. Some Bible scholars think that he was around twenty years old at that time. From what we can find in his life, Jeremiah wasn't formally educated into the priesthood like most priests. The Lord told Jeremiah that He, Himself, had ordained him! I'm sure as a young man, Jeremiah had doubts and insecurities, but he knew God had placed a call on his life. He knew that God had set him apart for an important prophetic ministry. I'm certain that assurance helped him when facing those hard and trying times. Do you know God's plan for your life? Have you felt there is something God is preparing you for? Oftentimes, life is confusing, and we can't fully understand what God's plans for our lives might be. We need God's wisdom when dealing with trials in our lives. No one enjoys hardships, but unfortunately, a lot of times, we only learn through hard times. Plus, it's during the hard times that our faith grows! When we realize that the difficulty is bigger than we are, that it's more than we can handle, we cry out to God for help. Remember, if you are God's child, He has a purpose for all He does or all He allows to come into our lives. He will always use the trials we go through as a way for us to help others.

"I've heard this question asked hundreds of times. 'Pastor, why do bad things happen to good people?' First of all, let me start by saying, there are no *good* people. None of us are good. Luke 18:19 tells us that none is good, save one, that is God. Now the answer to that question is simple. When God created humans, He gave them free will. We have lived in a fallen, sinful, evil world ever since Adam and Eve used that free will and chose to disobey God's perfect plan for their lives. Human's free will choices have made the world evil. That's where we live today, in a fallen world where bad things happen to everyone, law-abiding citizens or criminals. The only way to have any influence in this world is to have faith in God and pray to him for help. He listens to our prayers. He moves on our behalf. That doesn't mean we will never experience hardships or sorrow. But we can use our experiences, good or bad, as a testimony of how God was there and helped us. We can say I have been there, and this is how I made it through. We all have trials. How you deal with the trial is the key to success or failure.

"Psalm 139:14, 'I will praise thee; for I am fearfully and wonderfully made. Marvelous are your works, and I know this very well.' When we realize God made us and He has a plan for us, it helps us to go through the trials life throws at us. Jeremiah 29:11 lets us know God has a plan for us. 'For I know the thoughts I have toward you, saith the Lord, thoughts of peace, and not of evil, to give you an expected end.' Have you ever wondered what someone thought of you? Well, God tells you exactly what His thoughts are toward you. He wants you to have peace, and He has a future in mind for you. Isn't it reassuring to know that we have God watching over us and that He knows all about us? Isaiah 55:12 tells us, 'For my thoughts are not your thoughts, neither are your ways my ways, saith the Lord. For as the heavens are higher than the earth, so are My ways higher than your ways, and My thoughts higher than your thoughts. For as the rain cometh down, and the snow from heaven, and returneth not thither, but watereth the earth, and maketh it bring forth and bud, that it may give seed to the sower, and bread to the eater: So shall My word be that goeth forth out of my mouth: It shall not return unto me void, but it shall accomplish that which I please, and it shall prosper in the thing whereto I send it. For ye shall go out with joy, and be led forth with peace: the mountains and the hills shall break forth before you into singing, and all the trees of the fields shall clap their hands.'

"One of the most familiar scriptures we can find written on plaque today is Jeremiah 29:11. 'For I know the plans I have for you, declares the Lord, plans to prosper you and not harm you, plans to give you hope and a future.' God has a plan for every person ever born. But only those who put their trust in Christ will be able to fully know how to follow God's perfect plan for them. Does that mean that everything will go perfectly with no problems? Of course not! Life isn't perfect. Life is messy and full of problems. We live in an imperfect world, among imperfect people, and like I said earlier, every person born has free will. They can choose to use that will for good or evil! There will always be struggles and trials we have to face. But for those of us who have the Holy Spirit living with us, we can have faith that God will help us with those trials, and He promises in

Romans 8:28 that things will work out for our good. 'And we know that all things work together for good to them that love God, to them who are the called according to his purpose.' You may be thinking, What about me? I'm too old to do anything for God now. All I can say to that is, if you're still breathing, God has a reason for keeping you here. You need to ask Him what His will is for you now. Every time you wake up, alive on this earth, means God isn't finished with you yet. He still has a work that only you can do.

"Now after you leave the service today, take some time to talk with God. Ask Him to make it clear to you what His plan is for your life. Be fully aware that since you are alive, He had a plan in mind for you before He began forming you into the human you are today. Just like God made the world and the beautiful garden before He made Adam, God had a plan and a future for you before He placed you in the world! Don't ever forget that! Don't you think it's important for us to find out what God had in mind when He decided to create each one of us? Can't you see that the body, the mind, and the personality he gave each individual fit perfectly for the plan He had for the life He was creating? I don't know about you, but I've felt that important since the day I accepted Christ as my Savior. I ask Him regularly what His plan is for me. Even when you know part of the plan, you only get it in small doses. I know God has placed a call on my life to preach the gospel. But His plan for each of us is far above what our human minds can fully accept. He gives it to us as we are ready to receive it.

"When I first felt the call to preach, God didn't tell me I would be preaching in a castle twice every Sunday, having Bible study every Wednesday night with hundreds of people from all over the world. In the beginning, God never told me there would be important people at the castle services hearing me share the gospel with them. At the beginning of my calling, God never revealed to me the fact that the Dannaher ladies would offer me a full-time pastoral lodging here in this amazing castle, so I would be available for all the guests who might need counseling. God lets us know what his plan is one step at a time. Once we obey and follow through with each step he gives, he then tells us the next step. You may ask, Pastor John, how am I supposed to hear God? I'm so glad you asked. Everything God says or does is through the Holy Spirit, through prayer, and through the meditation on His Word.

"Psalm 119:105 tells us, 'Thy word is a lamp unto my feet, and a light unto my path.' As you study and meditate on His Word and you are asking for His leadership and guidance, you will hear and know His will for your life. Only then will you feel the peace and joy of living life to its fullest!" If God hasn't made it clear to you what his designed plan is for your life, follow this verse until he opens up the next door: "Whatsoever thy hand findeth to do, do it with thy might for there is no work, nor device, nor knowledge, nor wisdom, in the grave whither thou goest" (Ecclesiastes 9:10). This is talking about finding something you're talented at that you could do for God.

*****

After the service, as Jodi slowly walked back toward the aunts' living quarters, her young mind was whirling with thoughts about what she had just heard. The boys came up to where she had stopped, waiting for her family to catch up with her. The church services were inside the castle, but that wasn't saying it was in the next room. It was, in fact, many, many rooms, halls, and then more rooms away! Quite a distance. These days, the aunts had a small indoor scooter to get from one end of the castle to another. Jodi understood why. It could be a major workout to walk the full length of the square footage of that massive building and take a lot of time as well! On one of her other visits with her aunts, Jodi remembered Coleen telling her that the castle had over sixty-five thousand square feet and over a thousand rooms on the first and main floor. That didn't include the basement or the other eleven stories! The castle was large enough to accommodate a small city! Reggie got to Jodi before the other two boys. His energy in Ireland seemed to be what a teenage boy's energy should be. Not sluggish at all.

"Hey, Jodi, you want to go fishing off the shore behind the castle today? We're going out there right after lunch and thought you might enjoy going to watch the waves." Jodi smiled and agreed that would be fun. She noticed that Reggie was doing so much better with his allergies. He hadn't sneezed at all while in Ireland. The sea breeze must be the difference. He was vibrant and alert. Jodi had never seen him this way. It was great to see him fully enjoying his life for a change.

Aunt Coreen had Maribelle make the kids a picnic lunch so they could get started with their fishing. "The evening services will be here in the blink of an eye, and you kids, *especially you, boys,* will need to freshen up a bit before returning to the chapel." Jodi knew that would be the case, for sure. Those boys couldn't understand the full meaning of smelly. The kids asked Maribelle and the others if anyone else would like to join them, to which they all declined because of various reasons. Maribelle wanted to read over some recipes she wanted to keep in her files in hopes of enticing the aunts into allowing her more responsibility in the kitchen. She had a plan to show the ladies how much easier their life would be if she was in charge of all things related to the kitchen. The aunts regularly took naps between services, and the others planned a leisurely day, reading books in the library and napping as well. So off to the coastline the kids went with their gourmet picnic lunch. Johnny sat near Jodi, and Roman followed close behind him.

"Jodi, me and the guys were talking last night. We heard you talking about that strange dream you had and bits and pieces of the interpretations. Would you mind if we tagged along with you on your daily visits to the zoo? We'd feel better if you had someone with you, you know, just in case of an emergency."

Jodi giggled a little, thinking it really wasn't necessary. "There's always someone around when I'm there. Waylon and that other man are there almost every day. Of course, they're usually occupied with arguing. Either Evan, the elephant keeper, or some of the grounds people are there at some point during my visits. Usually, there is always someone in the ticket booth right in front of the entrance gate. But then again, things have changed a little. I'm visiting more inside these days because of the cold. Are you guys sure you won't get bored going there so often?" Jodi looked them over, searching their faces to see if they were being honest with her. "Johnny, I know you and Reggie go to the public library almost every day, studying the local plants and herbs, and, Roman, you go with them to study up on the local laws and such. When you get back to the castle, you are all staying in the library here, studying as though you have exams. I've heard all three of you making comments on how many interesting things you've discovered from the antique books in the castle's library and how different the plants and laws were here compared to the mountain. You going along with me will hinder all that. I know those studies are important to y'all, or you wouldn't be spending so much time doing it. Are you quite sure you want to sacrifice your study time to go to the zoo every day?"

Reggie plopped down on the opposite side of Johnny. "We're sure. Besides, we're part of a JR investigative team. That's what we do. Remember? Plus, we've spent the biggest part of our visit here looking at bushes and weeds or indoors. It's time we branch out and see the sites of Ireland."

Jodi felt a sweet, comforting feeling knowing her cousins wanted to make sure she was safe. Jodi quietly thanked God for her loving cousins. "Okay then, you're welcome to come along with me, and I'm thankful to have cousins like you."

Reggie nudged Johnny in his ribs with his elbow, teasing him, "That includes you, too, Johnny. Now you're stuck with us, thick-n-thin."

They had a good hearty laugh, and Johnny blushed slightly, honored that they acknowledged his place in their family. He was no longer the outsider in their little group.

*****

Pastor John had begun the evening services with the same lesson as the morning's lesson.

"God knew we would be bombarded with problems, so He gave us promises to help encourage us. So tonight, I'm going to make the sermon short and only give you scriptures to encourage you. Take them home and meditate on them. Hide them in your heart for when trying times come into your life. I hope you all have a pen and paper with you. If you don't, there should be some in the book caddy on the back of the bench in front of you. It's important that you take notes tonight. Write these verses down and read them often. Just because God has a plan for our life doesn't mean everything will run smoothly. We have an enemy that wants to destroy our peace, our success, and our effectiveness in bringing others to God. The devil will fight us every waking minute we breathe and even while we sleep! These promises of God will help you stay focused on who is in charge if we will keep our trust in God!

"John 16:33, 'These things have I spoken unto you, that in me ye might have peace. In the world ye shall have tribulation: but be of good cheer; I have overcome the world.'

"We are all fully aware that life equals problems. There's no way around that ugly fact! But the children of God have a great problem solver. All He requires is believing in Him and exercising faith in Him. He never promised a life without problems. He only promised to help those who believed in Him and asked for His help.

"Isaiah 41:10, 'Fear thou not; for I am with thee: be not dismayed; for I am thy God: I will strengthen thee; yea, I will help thee; yea, I will uphold thee with the right hand of my righteousness.'

"Philippians 4:6–7, 'Be careful for nothing; but in everything by prayer and supplication with thanksgiving let your requests be made known unto God. And the peace of God, which passeth all understanding, shall keep your hearts and minds through Christ Jesus.'

"Have you ever noticed that when worries and problems come into your life, your mind begins to stress? When that happens, your thinking automatically gets foggy. It's more difficult to think clearly. God tells us not to be anxious about anything. He will help us. Stay calm and depend on Him to help you.

"Psalm 34:4–5, 8, 'I sought the Lord and he heard me, and delivered me from all my fears. They looked unto him, and were lightened: and their faces were not ashamed. O taste and see that the Lord is good: Blessed is the man that trusteth in him.' [Trust him so you can experience his goodness in your life.]

"Taste and see that the Lord is good. Every child of God has tasted or experienced the goodness of God in their life. God is good to everyone. However, only His children know it is God's goodness. The rest of the world thinks of their daily blessings as something they achieve with their own skillfulness. Never once questioning where the blessing of that skillfulness actually comes from.

"Joshua 1:9, 'Have not I commanded thee? Be strong and of a good courage; be not afraid, neither be thou dismayed: for the LORD thy God is with thee whithersoever thou goest.'

"We tend to forget that God never leaves us! He is always where we are! That can get uncomfortable when you realize God is there, even when you are being ugly and sinful. If we would remember that reality of God's all-seeing eyes, I honestly believe it would change the way Christians live their daily lives!"

Jodi wrote every verse down in her journal. She knew that she needed those verses to keep her focused on God's protection. Her strange dream had made her fully aware of that need. She would be reading those scriptures and meditating on them, just like Pastor John suggested.

10

The group of four kids went to the zoo every day and had become quite close to the elephant family. The boys admitted that they were an intelligent group of animals and rather entertaining. They could understand now Jodi's fascination with them. One could easily start to think of them as almost human in their interactions with them. Evan was happy to see more young people coming to visit his elephants. He could see a big difference in the way the elephants felt, and their energy was much more vibrant. It was plain to see that the animals enjoyed the visits as much as the kids. They were active and energetic. The elephants seemed to be joyful and played more often even when the young group wasn't around. It's as if they knew the kids would return the next day. This knowledge also brought with it apprehension, worry, and sadness for Evan. Evan knew those elephants would mourn when the group of young people, especially Jodi, failed to show up for an extended period of time. It would feel like a death to them. Even knowing this, Evan didn't have the heart to stop the group from visiting them. It might possibly help the elephants by stopping the visits sooner, but there was no guarantee about that because Jodi had already been visiting them for a month. The connection, the fondness of her visits, had already bonded them to her. Evan loved his elephants. He had cared for them every day for years. He also loved and belonged to the One who created them. He had been praying for God to intervene in the feelings of both Jodi and the elephants. It was certain that he had no clue how to solve this situation for the best of all involved. Only God could do that.

*****

On the next day's visit, the sun was beaming bright and warm. The elephants were restless and eager to be outdoors. Just as Jodi and her cousins came through the entrance gate, the elephants were charging through their doors with gusto. Toby noticed Jodi right away and ran straight toward her! The kids laughed at the happy baby elephant. It was evident to all there that Toby loved Jodi a great deal! The baby interacted with the boys as well, but she returned to Jodi and didn't stay away from her for very long.

Johnny whispered to Roman, "Those two men are here on a regular basis. I think there may be something off about them. They seem angry most of the time. Does that seem logical for a working relationship?" Roman agreed it was odd behavior and remarked that he had also noticed the men arguing. Johnny continued, "You and Reggie stay here, close to Jodi. I'm going to get a little closer to see if I can hear anything they're talking about."

Roman cautioned Johnny, "They might notice you and become suspicious. I find it strange they haven't already been more guarded around us! They argue as though we are invisible. They act as though there's no one around to witness their odd behavior."

Johnny was watching the men while Roman was talking to him, then replied, "Well, there is a good distance between this habitat and the one they are next to. Anyway, you know how it is with most adults, especially men. Kids are invisible! They never pay any attention to what we are doing. They don't think we are intelligent enough to understand what's going on around us." Roman was glad Jodi was preoccupied with the energetic Toby and hadn't noticed their whisperings. He casually wandered over to where Reggie was talking with Mali, the grandmother elephant.

"Johnny has a suspicion about those two men over there. He's getting closer to investigate the situation. Help me keep Jodi's mind on the elephants." Reggie quietly laughed. "That's like asking me to make sure she continues to breathe regularly. Surely, you know that nothing else ever grabs her attention when she's visiting Toby! That's the real reason we bother coming here every day. Jodi wouldn't notice danger around her as long as those elephants were in her vision! But I agree, those two are up to something. They are here often. I know that Waylon works here, so obviously, he would be here, but who is the other guy? I have never seen him working on anything. Wasn't he one of the servers at the wedding dinner? Maybe they both work here too. Since they pick this same spot every time, maybe they have nothing to hide. It's possible we're reading more into it than there really is. I heard Waylon only comes during the day to check to see what fences need repairs, so he knows what will be needed for the shift that night. It would be a good idea to find out who that other man is and why he is constantly angry and fussing at Waylon. It is definitely worth looking into."

Johnny leisurely wandered in the direction of the two men. He remained on the side of the elephant habitat, not to alert suspicion. Continuing to offer the elephants hay, he listened with all his might to hear anything being said.

At last, Waylon became furious and yelled angrily, "I said I couldn't do what you're asking! I agreed to make it easier for you to cause the family trouble, and I've done that, with great regret and shame, I might add! You swore to me you wouldn't harm anyone! You said you were going to help cater at the wedding, only to get a close look at the family and the castle. Then we told you not to come. Your plan was called off, and you showed up anyway! You lied, and it almost cost my sister her life! I hate myself for letting you stay that day. I've told you all I know about the contents of the castle. I've given you the estimates of their value. But I refuse to help you by putting any of them in harm's way! They are, after all, my distant relatives! I will see if I can get the chance to give you the opportunity to talk with Jodi alone. She comes here every day, so that shouldn't pose a problem, and it is a public place. However, I don't see how a young girl can help you any. She can hardly persuade her family into doing anything they feel isn't right. You can threaten me all you want to, but I will not be a part of the rest! I realize I owe you a fortune. You'll get your money, but I cannot, and I will not do any more than that!" Waylon kicked the metal fence and walked away. Angry and sullen.

The other man, just as angry and sullen, stood there, staring at Waylon walking away. Reggie was watching the man. He and Mali were standing directly opposite the other man, and Reggie was glad that Mali hid him from the man's view. That gave Reggie a great opportunity to watch him closely. He noticed the man turn and glare at Jodi! What on earth could his interest be in her? Could it be the unusual interaction between the elephant and the girl? No, because the look the man had in his eyes was far from curiosity. The look he was giving Jodi was even more angry than it had been toward Waylon!

Johnny rejoined the two boys. "I believe that man talking with Waylon has been threatening him! Waylon just told him he would not and could not do what the man was asking of him. I didn't hear what that was, but it appeared to be a demand more than a request!"

Libby wandered over to where Toby was playing with Jodi. She seemed to be trying to get her baby to go back inside, so Jodi realized it was time for the visit to end. Seemed to Jodi that all mothers were the same. The kids could play together, but when it was nap time or time to eat, ready or not, playtime was over.

Reggie quickly told the guys what he had witnessed while Jodi was occupied, "Guys, I saw that other man staring toward Jodi, and it wasn't friendly! He appeared livid! Now I don't have a clue as to why that would be the case, but I'm starting to feel like *he* could be the reason for Jodi's warning in her dream!"

*****

The following morning, the castle was, once again, bombarded with knocks on the castle doors.

Mansfield answered immediately, "Hello, uh…Mr. Fahy, wasn't it? How may I help you this morning?" It was obvious that Mansfield was not eager to receive Waylon into the castle.

Waylon could sense his hesitation, so he hurriedly stated the reason for his visit. "I'm here to visit my sister. Is she available this morning?"

Mansfield pointed to the back of the castle. "Miss Maribelle has moved to the fisherman's cottage at the back of the castle. Just follow the stone path. It will take you straight to her."

Waylon thanked Mansfield and left.

Jodi had awakened earlier than usual. She got started on her devotional right away. She wanted to read over the passages of Scripture the preacher had mentioned but didn't have the time to fully discuss them with the congregation. He had told the congregation to read them later. She read over all those verses and decided to include a few more her aunt Hattie had given her after she interpreted her dream. Aunt Hattie had encouraged her not to think any more about the dream—to put it out of her mind until God chose to say more about it. So Jodi had tried her best to do just that.

Jodi turned to Matthew 6:31–33. "Therefore, take no thought saying, what shall I eat? Or, what shall I drink? Or, wherewithal shall we be clothed? For after all these things do the Gentiles seek: for your heavenly Father knoweth ye have need of these things. But seek ye first the kingdom of God and his righteousness; and all these things shall be added unto you."

Jodi understood quite well that God did know what she needed, and she trusted Him completely. She had heard it preached regularly that God wants us to believe in Him and come to Him with the faith and expectancy of an innocent child—the same way that child looks to its earthly father to give what is being asked for. She often thought about a story she once heard her pastor tell about a preacher's family during one of their family bedtime prayers. It was a regular thing for the family to watch a Western show called *Bonanza*. In this particular show, the character, Little Joe's horse, was sick or hurt. It must have been a continued show because, at the end of the show, the horse was still not well. During the family prayer that night, the baby of the family, around four or five years old, prayed that God would heal Little Joe's horse. Like most of us, the request was funny to the mother and siblings, and they were unable to completely hide their stifled snickers. The dad, a pastor, was upset about the laughter and chided them for snickering. He fully understood that the baby did not know the difference between a show and reality and was going to the only one who could make a difference in that horse's life! Jodi opened her prayer journal, where she had written what her pastor said after telling the story about the childlike faith.

Luke 18:16, "But Jesus called them unto him, and said, Suffer the little children to come unto me, and forbid them not: for such is the kingdom of God. God expects us to come to Him the same way. Once we become mature, we feel we are too old to ask God for the simple things in life. But God is interested in every detail of our life!"

Proverbs 3:5–6, "Trust in the Lord with all thine heart; lean not unto thine own understanding. In all thy ways acknowledge him and he shall direct thy paths."

Jodi made it a regular practice to depend on God to let her know what she needed to do. She depended on God's direction in her life. She had often been teased by others when they heard her randomly talk with God about things that were considered unimportant. But it was very natural for Jodi to talk with God about everything in her life. Just as she would a friend or family member standing with her at the time. To her, God was no different. She knew God was there with her all the time. Because she was aware of His constant presence, Jodi was equally grateful for God's mercy and forgiveness when she disappointed Him.

Romans 15:13, "Now the God of hope fill you with all joy and peace in believing, that ye may abound in hope, through the power of the Holy Ghost."

Psalms 94:18–19, "When I said, my foot slippeth; thy mercy, O Lord, held me up. In the multitude of my thoughts within me thy comforts delight my soul."

Jodi remembered her pastor from her church in Texas saying, "God never keeps a record of how many times his children slip up and fall. When we ask God to forgive us of the sins we commit and our shortcomings, He forgives, and He forgets! He never remembers them again!" Jodi was glad her pastor had suggested his congregation write the verses down. She had kept them in her journal and found them to be exactly what she needed.

Micah 7:19, "He will turn again, he will have compassion upon us; he will subdue our iniquities; and thou wilt cast all their sins into the depths of the sea." It was fascinating to Jodi how the Bible verses Pastor John and Aunt Hattie had given her went along with the verses she had written years ago in her journal.

Matthew 6:14–15, "For if ye forgive men their trespasses, your heavenly Father will also forgive you: But if ye forgive not men their trespasses, neither will your Father forgive your trespasses."

Jodi pondered on the Bible verses and was thankful God was there for her to depend on. "Father God, thank You for picking me up when I fall short of Your plans for me. Thank You for not allowing my failures to define who I am! Thank You for loving me, guiding me, and protecting me. Father God, I'm so thankful for the gift of the Holy Spirit. Please forgive me for how little I have let the Holy Spirit manifest the presence of Jesus in my life. Father, give me the understanding to know how to prepare my heart to respond to the Holy Spirit. I want to open my whole being to Him. I want to be filled with the Holy Spirit that I may be under His control so He can have the power to reveal Christ through me, so others will know who God is. In Jesus' name, amen."

As Jodi finished her morning prayer, she heard another knock at the castle's front doors. "Goodness, what a busy morning for Mansfield!" She decided to leave through the back doors so as to not disturb the visitors at the front doors. Her cousins were already outside, enjoying the fair weather. "Are you boys coming with me to the zoo this morning?"

Johnny answered her with enthusiasm, "Absolutely, you bet. You know, we kinda got attached to those elephants of yours. They're really something special."

Jodi giggled happily as the four of them headed out toward the zoo.

*****

Meanwhile, back at the castle, the visitor was there to speak with Sean. Mansfield told Sean he had a visitor. Sean left the morning paper on the ottoman in front of the chair where he had been sitting and reading. He went to see who it was calling him so early. "Governor! What a surprise! What brings you to our little part of the world?"

Sean's caller was none other than the Tennessee Governor!

"I know you must be shocked to see me here, Sean, of all places, right? I'm here, keeping my word to you and your family to haunt that evil man known as mayor. Well, believe it or not, the trail has brought me here! He is in your hometown, and he owns several casinos here. I have it on good authority that he is keeping a close eye on your family these days. I felt it important that you and your family know. I understand they are here visiting for the holidays?"

Sean was visibly upset by what he had just heard. "Yes, Governor, they are. You have reason to believe that he is watching our family and they are in danger?" Sean motioned for the governor to come into the library to sit.

The governor continued to talk as they walked to the library, "Without a doubt, young man! He's full of evil and out for revenge. He's watching your family, and that's not good!" Sean motioned for the governor to sit in a chair close to the fireplace. The governor walked to the chair and sat down, never stopping his conversation. "I would suggest that you keep everyone close in. Preferably here at the castle or on the castle grounds as much as possible until I can get a better understanding of his connections and his intentions. Of course, I'm limited in what I can do here in Ireland, so I regret to say the responsibility falls on your shoulders. My hands are basically tied. So far as I can tell, he has unlimited funds because of his businesses here, and he has some equally deep pockets and sponsors in other people. I'm supposing a lot of influential people owe him a large sum of money in gambling debts. He doesn't appear to have very many friends though. From what I've learned thus far, most people despise him! Not a big surprise. From what I have learned about him, that feeling is understandable. Oh, also, he isn't a mayor. That's only a nickname. I've discovered he acquired that *title* by having so many politicians in his back pocket. Gambling debts. It's a joke among all the ones who are in debt to him. He carries the name with pride. Well, I've said what I came to say. I must leave now and continue gathering information. I fully intend to bring this man to justice. I'm talking with one of the judges here. He is looking into pressing charges, so the wheels of justice are turning! If not in my courts in Tennessee, then here in his hometown! So far, I have only been able to find out that he is, in fact, watching your family. He hasn't done anything illegal that can be proven as yet, but I'm watching him like the Indian chief's hawk! When he does slip up, I have a judge that promises to put the cuffs on him! I'm sorry to say, that's about all legally I'm at liberty to do. I'm here on a holiday break, so I will be going back home this coming weekend. Until then, you and your family stay safe! Good day, Sean, and my best wishes and prayer for safety to you and your family."

The governor left the castle, and Sean set out to inform the rest of the family what he had learned. To his horror, Jodi and her cousins had already left for their daily visit to the zoo! After talking to the family, Carl called all the kids' cell phones in hopes of getting the kids back home. He wasn't able to get any of them to answer their phones, so he called the zoo. This was an emergency bordering on a crisis level!

11

odi and the boys were relaxing on the bench, where Jodi sat during all her visits. She was reading her daily devotional book, *365 Days of My Father's Blessings to You: From the King of King's Daughter.* Jodi got encouragement from reading God's promises every day. She took comfort in knowing that God Himself had instructed for those promises to be written for all His children. She claimed all the ones she felt were especially pertaining to her each day. The boys were watching the elephants and keeping an eye out for the two men. So far, they were nowhere to be seen. Jodi continued reading while pretending to ignore Toby. It had become a daily ritual with them. She often wondered if Toby would feel slighted if that little game were to stop. Lo and behold, just at that moment, Waylon came running around the corner of the elephant habitat, waving his arms, panting out of breath from his running. Here was the chance he needed to get Jodi alone so the overbearing man he was indebted to could talk privately with her.

"Boys, there's a phone call for you in the office. If you all will follow me, I'll show you where it is."

Jodi started to rise and follow, but Waylon quickly stopped her. "No, there's no reason for you to interrupt your visit with the elephants. The call is for the boys."

Jodi sat back down and resumed her reading, but the boys felt uncertain about leaving her there alone. Roman spoke up, "Reggie, Johnny, you two don't need to go. I'll go see who's calling."

Waylon stepped in, "The call is for all three of you boys."

Waylon's persistence on all three of them leaving annoyed the boys and made them suspicious as well. Johnny was a young man of only seventeen, but he was an impressive six-foot-four and stood towering over Waylon. "Only one person can answer the phone, so I'm sure one person will be adequate to answer the call!" Johnny's position as a cornerback for his school football team had caused him to be lean and mean when faced with opposition. He was a professional when it came to running defense for his team or, in this case, his cousin and his friend! The Tennessee University saw his potential and sought him out, offering him their athletic scholarship for football. He knew how to take care of opposition!

The look in Johnny's eyes told Waylon that he was a guy who enjoyed hand-to-hand combat and relished the opportunity to prove he survived and thrived each time! Johnny had used such a force in his tone that Waylon didn't push the issue any further, only turned to take Roman to the phone. Roman sent Johnny a half-crooked grin with a comical salute then ran to see what the call was all about. Waylon and Roman had no more gone out of sight when the other strange man came into view. He and Waylon were usually seen together. But here he was alone, and it appeared he was coming in their direction. Johnny noticed and started back toward Jodi because that was the direction the man was headed. Unfortunately, the man reached Jodi first. Johnny and Reggie were on the other side of the fence. The gruff man grabbed Jodi by the arm, jerking her from off the bench! Jodi was totally taken aback by the sheer shock of being violently jerked from off her seat! She let out a scream and dropped her devotional book to the ground! As soon as her eyes saw her attacker's face, Jodi recognized him as the man she had witnessed regularly arguing with Waylon.

Psalm 46:10 popped into her mind. "Be still and know that I am God: I will be exalted among the heathen, I will be exalted in the earth." Jodi instantly felt an overwhelming peace come over her. Johnny and Reggie came close to them and grabbed the man by his two arms. They had a counterattack planned for Jodi's attacker. The elephants were trumpeting loudly! Stomping the ground in anger! The three adult elephants were pounding and pushing on the gate, trying desperately to get to Jodi! They had heard her scream and responded to her fear. All that happened within a tenth of a second, but it seemed to Jodi to be happening in slow motion! She was totally focused and thinking clearly. The man growled and hissed like a madman, jerking his arms free from the two boys' grasp, taking them by surprise, elbowing them both with a martial art's *Krav Maga* move, knocking Johnny off balance and to the ground! The violent blow to Johnny's stomach had knocked the wind out of him! He lay on the cement ground, gasping for breath! The man raised his arm high and hit Reggie with a massive blow to his nose! Reggie had blood pouring from his nose and streaming down his face! Johnny quickly recovered, got back to his feet, and reached to punch the man, but Jodi shook her head *no*. She saw how quickly her cousins had been caught off guard and hurt. She didn't want anything more to happen to them. She knew in her heart that this was what her dream had warned her about. This situation was between the attacker and her!

Jodi looked straight into the man's eyes and asked, "Who are you, and what do you want with me?"

The man pulled Jodi by her arm, tightening his grip to a painful degree, drawing her closer to his face, and growled fiercely, "I'm going to make your family pay for all they have cost me! I'm going to take you somewhere, where you will never be seen again!" He grabbed Jodi's arm again, this time tightening his grip even harder. Jodi stood her ground. She was tougher than she appeared. Jodi was surprised at how solid her feet remained planted to the ground and unmoved with no effort of her own! The man had a difficult time moving her very far. Both Johnny and Reggie tried pushing their way between the man and Jodi. Jodi put up her hand, indicating to her cousins not to intervene just yet. She didn't feel afraid for herself, but she did feel concerned for her cousins. Poor Reggie was bleeding, and Johnny was coughing from the massive blow to his stomach! "Absalom, you can't take me away…"

The man stared at Jodi as if she was crazy. "Why did you call me Absalom? That's not my name! Are you insane?"

Jodi still felt a great calmness. She felt no fear. The reasoning in her mind told her it was God keeping her calm. "No, I'm sure that isn't *your* name. I'm speaking to the spirit from which your actions are coming from."

This confused the man and angered him even more. He reached into his pocket and withdrew a gun. He was totally bewildered as to why he was unable to move such a small young girl! Pointing the gun toward the boys, he continued trying to drag Jodi away. She held firm to her place, still with no effort on her part. The man wasn't able to move her. Jodi seemed relaxed, and that unnerved the man. Being a young girl, she found the situation so strange that she let out a slight giggle, feeling surprised by the odd situation. She had never experienced anything like it before!

The man was bewildered and started shaking her violently and asked, "Why are you so calm? What are you giggling about? Don't you have sense enough to understand I can shoot you and these boys?"

Jodi simply said, "You can't do that either."

"What or who in the world is going to stop me? How can you be so sure I won't shoot you here and now just to prove my point?"

"Because my Father told me He would take care of me, and Absalom himself admitted he could not harm me."

"Who is this Absalom you keep mentioning? What has he to do with any of this?" He shoved the boys back out of the way. The man was deceptively strong. He appeared to be short and weak, but his martial art training helped him to control the boys. He had caught them off guard and got the upper hand for the first blow! The two boys had different outlooks on the situation they were in. Johnny was trying to be cautious and not appear too threatening, seeing the man had a gun, fearing the man might get nervous enough to shoot Jodi, but Reggie was frustrated from the pain in his throbbing nose and annoyed that Jodi kept putting them off.

Wiping the blood from his nose with his shirt sleeve, Reggie voiced his impatience, and his frustration was evident as he yelled at her, "Jodi, why are you stopping us? We can take this guy!"

After hearing Reggie's threat, the man became nervous and pointed the gun toward him! Jodi knocked the man's arm down toward the ground just as the shot was fired! The man lost control of the gun, and it flew out of his hand after the gunshot. The elephants were loud and angry! There was a major fuss being made! Their angry stomping and the autumn winds had caused a great dust storm, making it difficult to see clearly. Evan had heard the commotion the elephants were making, and the gunshot caused him great concern! He ran to investigate. Unable to see past the gate, he made the elephants move away from the gate so he could go inside with them. After getting the gate open, all four elephants charged through the open gate and around to where the boys were standing, ready to fight off Jodi's attacker! They stomped Evan's foot and broke it in their haste to get out. At the same time, all three of the kids were scrambling on the ground with the attacker, each trying to retrieve the fallen gun! With the thick dust filling the air, it wasn't possible to see. They were all feeling around on the ground for the gun. The attacker's hand reached it first and retrieved the gun. He stood up and proceeded to try to shoot Jodi.

Johnny and Reggie tackled the man, and several gunshots were heard. The man desperately tried to aim the gun toward Jodi! Reggie and Johnny had ducked down to a squatted position to avoid getting shot then jumped up to tackle the man again, but at that moment, the elephants came charging around and knocked them away from the man! At that very instant, the mother elephant, Libby, saw the gun and used her trunk to slap it out of the man's hand. In the process of that, the slap had knocked the man to the ground! Little Toby ran over and wrapped her trunk around Jodi's arm, standing between Jodi and her attacker! The attacker had been knocked out cold from the fall. The group gathered around, looking closely at the man who had tried to kidnap Jodi and then had attempted to kill them all. They had to fan the air with their arms, trying to clear the dust from the air so they could see more clearly. Johnny quickly retrieved the gun and emptied the contents. As the dust began to settle and it was possible to see again, they all noticed blood was running from the man's head onto the cement! He wasn't breathing, having hit his head on the cement. The fall had killed him! What a nightmare!

Roman returned back from the call to tell them they needed to return home because of the potential danger, only to find that the danger had already taken place and someone had been killed! Roman informed everyone that the man lying before them was none other than the mayor from the Tennessee can hunts! Jodi took in a huge, shocked breath. This man looked nothing like she had pictured in her mind. She had been told he was a dark, foreign man. She instantly made the connection between the dark, menacing bat in her dreams to her image of what she thought the man would look like. The darkness of his character was the obvious reason for the bat, but she now realized she had assumed the enemy would be darker inside and out. This man was definitely dark, but it wasn't a natural skin color. His coloring was from living in a tanning bed. He was almost orange. Wow, what a turn of events!

The chaos around them now was more staggering than the attempted kidnapping and shooting. An ambulance had arrived, and the authorities were throwing questions at the kids faster than they could answer. The evil mayor had waited for the employee at the entrance booth to go on their lunch break. He didn't know what day he would have the opportunity, but he knew the time because there were no witnesses to speak of! The lady working at the entrance booth informed the Ireland guards that the man had paid her to take an early lunch break and told her not to return for an hour! She said it wasn't a friendly request. The man had threatened her life if she refused to leave!

She continued talking to the police with her voice shaking and scared, "As soon as I left the paying booth, I called the police station." The officer in charge was writing everything down. Johnny had used his cell to call Jodi's dad, Andrew, Sean, and Carl. He then wondered why the call for them had not come to Reggie's or Roman's cell.

"Guys, why did you have to go to the zoo office to get the call? Why not one of your cells?"

Roman was embarrassed to admit the reason. "Dad gave me a good lecture about that. My ear is still throbbing from the verbal lashing he gave me!" Roman rubbed his right ear to emphasize the severity of the reprimand. "My phone had died, and Reggie had forgotten to bring his. Jodi had her ringer off so as to not scare the animals. She always turns it off before getting here, and no one at the castle had your number. They had no other choice but to call the zoo. Of course, they had no idea anything was happening today. They got a visit from the Tennessee governor this morning saying that the mayor was here and intended to do the family harm. Dad was calling to insist we come back to the castle. That's how I knew who the man was as soon as I saw him lying there."

The police had gathered all the information about where everyone was staying and told them not to leave Ireland until they were finished with the investigation.

12

Life appeared to go back to normal, with the exception of trying to save Toby and the other elephants from extermination. Jodi was earnestly praying for God to protect them. She and all her family felt the elephants should be rewarded for their bravery and treated with honor for their obvious part in protecting and saving the kids' lives! But like most people, the officials in charge felt that human life was more valuable than an animal's life, even if that human was more evil and vile than an animal could ever be and even if that same vile person was in the process of taking the lives of three children!

Since the terrible attempted kidnapping and death, the elephants had been acting up and not well behaved, which, for these elephants, was very abnormal. Their behavior had become increasingly moody, and they were not eating well. They were agitated. Jodi's inability to visit them made everything worse and affected them badly! It appeared to everyone who didn't know the character of the elephants that they had gone rogue! Evan came to the castle and shared with the family that it had become increasingly difficult to calm them down. They were in a constant state of agitation since the incident happened and especially since Jodi was no longer permitted to visit them.

As Jodi lay in her comfortable bed, her mind refused to let her sleep. Her thoughts kept going over and over the things she had heard Evan say when he came to visit them at the castle. Evan came to share with them his concern for his elephants' lives. He had informed the family that the elephants had been scheduled to be euthanized by the end of the year and pleaded with Sean, Andrew, and Carl to go to the judge to see if they could change things. There was only one month left remaining in the year, so time wasn't on their side!

Jodi tossed and turned in her bed, rehashing all that had happened and the possibilities of things that could still happen and wondering how to make everything work out well for the elephants. She sat up in her bed like a bolt of lightning had struck her! What had happened to her? This wasn't like her at all! Since when did she ever worry to this extent? The way she was acting was how one of her favorite preachers described as *practical atheism!* God promises all things will work for our good! Jodi went to the bay window and watched the crashing waves again. Her troubled mind marveled at how strange it was that the violently boisterous waves caused her to feel so calm and relaxed.

She opened her Bible to Romans 8:28. "And we know that all things work together for good to them that love God, to those who are called according to his purpose." Jodi placed her hand on the open page of her Bible as she looked back out to the sea. Yes, it was like atheism when we worry! It is like saying God isn't going to keep His Word! Things were extremely bad. Yes, that was a fact! But there was a bigger fact, a more important fact. God will work this bad situation out to be for the good. He promises that!

She bowed her head and prayed, "Father, forgive me for staying awake due to worry. Forgive me for not trusting You to care for Toby and her family. You sent me a dream to warn me of the potential danger ahead of time. You knew what would be taking place before it happened. You knew and probably instructed the elephants to protect me. Father, I know You set up, You instigated, my friendship with the elephants from the beginning because You knew what was going to happen, and You knew what would be needed to be done during that whole mess! You kept me at peace. I felt no fear at all during the whole attempted kidnapping! It was You that prevented that man from moving me! I know that was You, Father! So I am trusting that You have already got a plan on how to save these elephants who have obviously done what You wanted to be done. I'm trusting You to work out their safety. I am concerned about one thing. I'm concerned about not being able to visit with them and how confusing that must be for such sensitive animals. Please give their hearts and minds peace. In Jesus' name, amen."

Jodi went to her bed and fell into a quiet and peaceful sleep.

*****

The days were getting colder, and when the night started to set in, the winds coming off from the sea could chill you to the bone. The aunts had Maribelle leave before nightfall so she wouldn't get cold while going to the cottage. The aunts offered Maribelle the fisherman's cottage just a sidewalk distance from the castle so she could have some independence yet still be close enough for help and not so far away that she couldn't come to the castle daily to resume the duties in the kitchen that she had insisted taking on. She loved living at the cottage. It was cozy and had much more space than her tiny apartment. The family enjoyed having Maribelle in the castle with them, but they had the feeling Maribelle was uncomfortable being under their concerned and watchful eyes. They felt certain the cottage would give her more privacy and help her have peace of mind. Her moving to the cottage had nothing to do with the castle not having enough space. Quite the contrary! The aunts felt if she had her own private space, she might be more relaxed and heal faster. The little fisherman's cabin had a full view of the sea. It sat in the middle of a small island with only a walkway attaching it to the land. With windows on every wall, there wasn't much privacy, but Maribelle felt it was perfect for her.

At night, she could sit in the small living room with all the lights out and enjoy watching the beams of light from the attached lighthouse flickering on the waves of the sea. There was a small entrance from the front door that led to an open living room with an attached kitchen. A wood-burning fireplace in the middle of the main wall and windows on every other wall. There was one small bedroom and bathroom. The cabin was small, but it was much bigger than her tiny apartment, and Maribelle loved it! She was thankful to have the Dannaher family help her and was surprised by their generosity. She had never met anyone like them before! However, she wanted to do more. She still wasn't at her full strength, and that annoyed her! She noticed she was getting bored more easily. She wanted to get back to her usual routine, but her body refused to fully cooperate with all she wanted to do! She was reminded of the Bible verse she had heard in Sunday school as a young girl. The spirit is willing, but the flesh is weak. Maribelle was believing that verse, not only spiritually but literally!

She woke to a gloomy, rainy morning. Not that it made a big difference for her. She had been in a slump for over a month now. She had much more energy these days and wanted more to do. A major *lackluster* for life had become an everyday way of seeing the world around her. So boring was her life. She wondered why she bothered getting up at all. The few responsibilities the aunts had given her were minuscule at most. She needed more to keep her challenged these days. Although her energy was returning, and that was the cause of her wanting more to do, the main reason the aunts refused to allow her more responsibility was that newfound energy was short-lived and left fast, leaving her drained and pale from exerting herself. Maribelle understood this but felt too impatient to care how drained she felt afterward.

Maribelle now had the full story of how her *snakebite* came about. Waylon had told her the full story during his last visit. Ironically, it was the same day the evil mayor had tried to kidnap Jodi and had died because of his evil deeds. It was so strange it was hard to believe. She was concerned that the aunts, Sean, and Coleen would never believe such a wild tale! She knew in her heart that after all they had done for her, they had to be informed. It was all done by the evil mayor, who was now dead! Since she had been injected with that snake venom by that evil man, she had struggled to regain her ambition for life. Sure, the energy was slowly returning, but the ambition and drive were lacking in comparison to what it was before all this nightmare happened. She felt that more responsibilities in the castle's kitchen were just what she needed to pull her out of her slump. But first, she must tell the family the ugly truth of everything that had happened. Maribelle lay in her warm bed, listening to the rain falling on the metal roof of the cottage. She was trying to decide if there was a real need for her to even get out of bed.

Bam! Bam! Bam! Well, now she had to get out of bed because some rude person had made it clear they were at her doorway too early in the morning! Opening the door to the dreary, wet morning, Maribelle stared at the postman standing at her door, dripping wet from the rain. "Good morning, miss. I have a special delivery for you. Would you sign here, please?" The man handed Maribelle a slate to put her signature on. As she scribbled her name onto the paper, she wondered who on earth would be sending her a package. *A special delivery package!* Maribelle handed the signed slate over to the dripping wet delivery man. "Thank you, miss. Have a nice day." The postman ran back into the rain and jumped into his truck, then drove away.

Maribelle stood, staring at the small package, searching for the identification of the sender. There was no name and no return address. Strange, but at least she wasn't bored at the moment. She tore open the package and read the enclosed letter, "Maribelle, I am your uncle, your father's brother. I know you must be in shock to read that. Your dad probably never mentioned me to you. I can understand that. My line of business is somewhat dangerous, and anyone involved in my life usually doesn't live to regret it. However, if you are reading this letter, that means I am no longer living, and you, my dear unfortunate niece, are my next of kin. Since your brother is older, he would naturally be the next in line to receive this. It pains me to inform you of this, but he cannot inherit this because he is, in fact, one of the names on the enclosed list. You are an heiress to a large sum, along with the potential to make more…much more, should you choose to follow in my footsteps.

"Enclosed is a black book with the bank account of more than nine hundred ninety-eight million American dollars! Try your best not to spend it all in one place. Seriously, all joking aside, my lawyers have been instructed to change the money over into American dollars and open up an account in your name. I had planned to change the money over to American dollars myself, and if I live, I will do that. Changing the money is the easiest way to protect it from the hands who are desperate to get me and the money. Putting the money into an American account would be wise. Guard the book with your life! It is only a matter of time before it is discovered that you are the one who now has it. I would advise you to hire a bodyguard and stay alert! Trust no one! No, I'm not being overly dramatic! If you decide you want nothing to do with this, sign the money over to a charity of your choice and burn the book. That is the only way you can be sure of being safe. Should it ever be discovered that your name is attached to the money, you will be in danger! I've dealt with that danger since the day I started this job and gained its wealth over thirty years ago. If you are reading this now, well…the danger has caught up with me, and they will be searching for the book and the money!"

Maribelle had to sit in the chair closest to the door while reading the letter. She couldn't grasp all that she had read! An uncle? Nine hundred ninety-eight million American dollars! A black book. She opened the book with shaky hands. What could be in the book that someone was willing to kill to get it, and why was her brother's name in it? As Maribelle opened the book, she noticed it was full of names. Each name had a date out beside it, then another name after the date. Some of the names had sums of money after the date. Other names had crimes that those names were apparently involved in or responsible for. Then another sum of money signed *paid until next installment due.* It was all quite confusing. It appeared that the large sum of money had come from the people on the list being blackmailed, a sort of hush money, and others for payments for gambling debts. Just like the letter said, her brother, Waylon's name was among the list of debtors. Her dad's name had been among the debtors, but it had been crossed out because of his death. However, his debt wasn't going unpaid! It had, in fact, been added to her brother's debt. Five hundred thousand American dollars was the number listed after his name! No wonder he was having to deal with a man like the mayor. Waylon was being forced to get information to help sue the family and give the mayor access to owning the castle! And now here was a man claiming to be their uncle, also holding a large debt over her brother's head. Not only his debt but their dad's debt as well!

Closing the book and folding the letter, Maribelle noticed more writing on the back of the letter. "Maribelle, the book has names of people who have murdered and owe large sums of money in gambling debts. I have proof of all this, and you will, too, if you want it. It's all in a safe deposit box in the bank. Be careful, my dear girl! This isn't a game! There are further instructions, with the evidence in the safe deposit box, along with the name of a trusted bodyguard. This man has no idea who will be receiving this letter. He will be waiting to hear from whomever will be the next person in charge of the book and fortune. Should you choose not to continue in this line of work, he will simply look elsewhere for work. There is no need to inform him or contact him for any reason. The less people know you're involved, the safer you will be. It would be unwise to let him know who you are! This is the way I chose to live my life. You may not want this for yourself. All you have to do is walk away. Get rid of the money and burn the book! Signed, Brody Cormac."

Maribelle read the name over again, *Cormac*. She had never heard of any family with that name, yet this letter came from a man claiming to be her uncle, her dad's brother. How was that even possible? Her mother's maiden name was Dannaher. Her dad's name was Fahy. How on earth did Cormac fit in?

Maribelle sat in utter shock! Not ten minutes ago, she was mulling over the dreariness of her life. Now she had been offered a life in crime and danger! How could so much change within moments of waking up? Even before she had her first cup of coffee!

It was as obvious as the nose on your face that Maribelle had been given an answer to her prayer. It was a *huge* miracle! No one in a million lifetimes would have ever guessed a fortune would come to her and in this way! Maribelle had heard and fully understood why Jodi had been concerned and rightly so that Toby and her relative elephants were going to be put down because of their killing a man while protecting Jodi's life. Now there was money and means to relocate the elephants if they could come up with a place to keep them safe and secure. Maribelle decided she would talk with the family as soon as they all came to breakfast. This was the charity she would invest the hush-blackmail money in. However, she wasn't sure what to do about all the gambling debts. She decided she needed to talk it over with the family and get their view on the situation before making any final decisions.

First, though, she had to come clean on how the snakebite happened and why. That wasn't going to be easy, for she had grown to love this family, and now she considered them her family, which they were distant family, but family just the same. Maribelle got her phone to call her brother, Waylon. She had to have a serious and lengthy talk with him before telling the family at the castle everything!

13

Maribelle sat quietly at the breakfast table. She was thinking about the sermon she had heard the night before, wondering how God was going to help her…how He was going to turn all these bad things to her good. She was especially burdened by what she needed to talk with the family about. She was very thankful she had met them because she felt certain, had she not met them, she would have never understood the importance of the Bible and talking with God. This awful story had to be told! She had put it off too long already. She must tell them everything now! Jodi watched as Maribelle played with her food, moving it about with her fork.

"Maribelle, is something troubling you this morning? Aren't you feeling well?"

Maribelle looked up and appeared tired and pale. "Yes, there is something very serious troubling me, and I'm nervous about sharing it with any of you for fear you will hate me. I've grown to love you all. You've been so kind and generous to my brother and me. I feel I've betrayed your confidence by keeping this from you, and now I find myself in a situation I can't handle on my own. I need professional advice."

Sean, being the head of the castle and feeling responsible for Maribelle and her brother being involved with his family, was the first to respond to Maribelle's odd statement. "Maribelle, no matter what the situation is, our family could never hate you. Let's all go to the library so we can be more comfortable." The family all left the table and went across the foyer to the library. The warm fire was glowing from the fireplace, where Mansfield had started it hours

93

before the family had gotten up. Sitting comfortably and waiting for what seemed to be a heavy burden on Maribelle's mind, the family waited quietly for her to begin.

Sean, trying to help her be a bit more relaxed, said, "What is your trouble?"

The young lady looked sick with shame as she began to tell them her story, "My brother has a severe sickness of gambling. Our father and our grandfather before him had the same sickness. I've tried to reason with Waylon, but he never seemed to have the ability to stop himself. Hattie, the Bible verses you and Coreen read to me the first day I arrived here helped me to understand that this sickness is definitely a sin sickness of iniquity. It has been a sickness in our family for generations. When they start gambling or drinking, they don't seem able to stop. It becomes a fixation so strong that it controls every waking moment of their lives! I don't know how many generations have been afflicted with this, but it's been a long time, and it is rooted deep! I wasn't aware of how deep until I received a letter this morning, filling me in on what's happening to my brother. But more about that after I tell you how I came to be here." Maribelle had tears of shame glistening in her eyes as she spilled out the details of her brother's involvement in the crime. "The snakebite wasn't from an actual snake. It was from a device the mayor paid to have custom made from an iron cane with syringe needles made from real viper fangs coming out the end of it. He got the idea from the cane my brother always carries with him. Only Waylon's cane has a removable knife in it. The mayor saw it and had someone make what he needed to carry out his evil plan to hurt your family. He accumulated the venom from one of the vipers at the Reptile Zoo where my brother works. My brother gave him access to get it but had no idea at the time what he wanted it for. The man struck me with the venom at the wedding dinner in hopes of blackmailing your family into paying off my brother's debts and in hopes of creating your need to sell this castle, giving him access to purchase it and taking it away from you, all because of your family interfering with his planned can hunts on the mountain.

"When Waylon first told me of the man's plan, he had no knowledge of his plans to inject someone with the snake's venom. The man insisted on helping with the catering at the wedding, and Waylon thought it was so he could have access to see what all the castle had to offer him. Well, I refused to be a part of it, and Waylon agreed with me and told the man the deal was off! When the man showed up at the wedding anyway, we were both beside ourselves with stress. Not knowing what to do. We couldn't understand why he came uninvited under the disguise of one of my caterers. We didn't want to cause a scene, so we didn't say anything to him." Maribelle stopped talking to wipe away the tears that had started flowing down her cheeks.

Jodi's thoughts went back to the day of the wedding dinner and remembered how clumsy Waylon had been. Now she could easily understand why he appeared so distracted. Maribelle took in a deep breath then continued, "Neither of us knew the man had planned to inject me with the snake venom! Waylon had no idea what the man wanted the venom for. My brother has had to do favors for this man for years because of the debt he owes. I refused to be part of it, and Waylon had agreed to forget following through with it. It seems the mayor lied to us and followed through without our agreeing to help him. He told Waylon he used me as the target for the venom because we had refused to cooperate with him! Since Waylon usually did everything he was told, the man blamed me!"

The family sat in stunned silence. Why would a brother get his sister involved with someone as evil as that man? Maribelle could've had an allergic reaction from the venom, and even though she didn't, she still could have easily died! What a cruel way to seek revenge and pay off a gambling debt! Sean, obviously upset by what he had just heard, asked her, "The morning Waylon came to ask if we would take care of you, he appeared to be looking for something. Do you know what that was?"

Maribelle was even more embarrassed than before. Her pale cheeks were burning red and feverish. "He knew where to find what he was looking for. The mayor had discarded the metal device with the needles underneath the dining room drapes so it would not be discovered on him that night and demanded Waylon get it back before it was found by someone at the castle. He had that part of the cane with the fangs made so it could be easily ejected. When you noticed he was looking around, he was mentally appraising the value of your property. Another one of the mayor's demands. Waylon is not only a master welder and stonemason, but he also has a degree as a property appraiser and a realtor license. He's very intelligent, book-wise. But his gambling and drinking have caused him to become extremely foolish! Waylon owes this man a huge fortune that he can never repay. And now I find that he is in debt, an unbelievable amount, to a man claiming to be our uncle! Before you become sickened by our behavior, to the point that you can't hear anything further, let me be quick to say my brother has since asked me to forgive him for his stupidity and cruelness. He was overwhelmed by the mayor's constant threats to kill him if he didn't cause your family distress and holding his debts over his head. He wasn't thinking straight. He wants to ask your family's forgiveness as well but wasn't sure how to go about it. I wasn't sure how to go about that either until I received a letter this morning."

Maribelle reached into her pocket with a trembling hand and brought out a little black book. "I became a Christian as a young girl but have never grown in my walk with God. I never had anyone to guide me on how to go about learning the things I should know. I had no idea how important going to a Bible believing and teaching church was, and I didn't understand how important reading the Bible was. Since I have come into your home, I have a new way of understanding what God expects of me. Since becoming a Christian, I have had a guilty conscience on any and all things not pleasing to God in my life and have changed my actions when met with guilt. However, that is as far as my godly walk has flourished. I am grateful that your family has helped me know how to walk with and learn from God. Because of this awful shameful mess and since the death of the mayor, I've had a long talk with Waylon, and he has accepted Christ also. We are both very new to all this way of living and hope you can find it in your hearts to forgive us both." Maribelle handed the book to Sean, and he opened it to see what it was all about. After glancing over a few pages, he then gave the book to Andrew and told him to notice the names where crimes had been committed then added, "Notice the name signed at the end."

Turning his attention back to Maribelle, Sean said, "I can fully understand your dilemma here. It's difficult to have something this scary coming against someone you love. Even if that someone is being led by someone who is willing to risk his sister's life to get what he wants. However, we need to know what you plan to do about this option you have been offered. Do you plan on continuing your uncle's blackmail scheme, or are you asking for a legal way out?"

The room sat silent, holding their breath. The whole family cared for Maribelle and hoped she would make the right and moral decision.

"Well, frankly, I was hoping to suggest a solution that would make everyone happy and get me out of the danger pocket of this blackmail racket. Aside from the tithes and offerings due to the large sum I've acquired…see, I have learned quite a bit from the family. Tithes and offerings are newly acquired habits in my Christian walk. That's just one of the important things I knew nothing about." Maribelle then turned her attention to Carl. "Mr. Ryan, I have been hearing about your discussions with the mountain chief on reserving the land where the can hunts were trying to start for an elephant habitat. Did I hear you say there were over one thousand acres of natural forestland connected to the area where the shack once was?"

Carl nodded his head yes. "Actually, the chief of the mountain has generously donated over three thousand acres. The land has a sixty-two-foot waterfall where the water lands into a beautiful lake where the kids go fishing every summer."

"Oh how wonderful, that's amazing! Also, because the elephants are scheduled to be put down since they killed the mayor, I know you and Mr. O'Connor are negotiating a way to purchase the elephants from the Ireland Rescue Zoo and take them to the mountain. From what I understand, that is a large amount of money that would need to be borrowed. I would like to offer the money from this account for that cause. Mr. O'Connor could write up all the legal papers and set up and transfer the funds to the elephant foundation. With that fund, buy the elephants and the land, and have the rest put into an account to fund the care of the elephants for the rest of their lives. If there are any remaining funds after the death of all four elephants, then I'd like for the remaining funds to go to the old chief's safari camp I've heard the kids talking so much about. I would like to pay off each of the gambler's debts with the understanding that if they ever gambled again, their payment for the debt would be rescinded, and full payment would again be required by them. If everyone here agrees with that, I'd like for Mr. O'Connor to set that plan up with one of the banks here in Ireland, that the debt would return to them, and they would follow through with the collection of the debts. I have talked with my brother and told him all the details and plans. He has already begun his gambling and drinking counseling and is extremely grateful for another chance. He hopes to have a meeting with everyone here to apologize and mend the trouble he has caused."

The group was gobsmacked over the information handed to them. What a whirlwind of events!

Carl spoke up, "That's a very generous offer. I, for one, am grateful to you. There is no charge for the land. The chief held a council meeting, and it has been approved and already designated for the elephant habitat. They are building the fence and elephant house as we speak. We're trusting that the judge will see things our way and sell the elephants to us."

Sean turned his attention back to Maribelle. "You and Waylon are our cousins through your mother's bloodline. You were wondering how the man who wrote this letter could be your uncle and your dad's brother with a different last name. Well, our research shows that your dad changed his last name to Fahy before you or Waylon were born. That is why the man who sent you this book and letter is your uncle. Also, everything he said about the additional information in a bank safe deposit box is true. When the Tennessee governor was here, he came across that information when investigating the crimes of the man we know as mayor. Only we didn't have a clue where to find the list of names, the information was talking about… until now! Turns out, the mayor's name is *Brody Cormac!* That is how this *mayor* fella, the man threatening Waylon and the man claiming to be your uncle, the extortionist, are all one and the same man with a different last name! I was quite shocked when I read *Brody Cormac* at the end of that letter you showed me, because Brody Cormac is the evil man called mayor and your blackmailing uncle! When I knew all the details of this man's character, it was easy to understand why your dad would want to disown him and never mention him to his children! What isn't easy to understand is how an uncle could be so evil as to manipulate his nephew and try to kill the niece he left a fortune to in his will! The man was obviously insane!"

14

Waylon, true to what Maribelle had said about him, had come to ask the family for forgiveness and had shown great sincerity and humility. He cried tears of shame and remorse and found it difficult to look the family in the eye. Aunt Hattie was the first to find her voice. "My sweet children, Maribelle and Waylon, you are both forgiven. There's no question on that issue. You have both suffered far more than any of our family has experienced in this whole thing. Don't think another thing about it." Then the smiling, gentle old lady turned to her family and said, "Have I spoken correctly for everyone here?" Altogether, there was a resounding *yes!*

Hattie continued, "My great-nephew, Sean is the head of this castle and all that entails, but I am the head of Sean." She laughed a gentle laugh with a wink toward the group. "Having said that, I'd like to offer a job to our extended family, Maribelle and her brother, Waylon. Maribelle, you have been after us for weeks now to give you more responsibilities. How would you like to be the castle's full-time chef? That would require long hours of cooking and serving all our guests year-round and extra cooking and serving when the top floor has been rented out by very important people. We require amazing dishes and desserts on a daily basis. We have hired caterers up to this point, but we now feel the need to hire a full-time chef. Do you feel that is something you are up for and would enjoy?"

Maribelle's face spoke volumes, and no words were necessary, but she speedily said, "Yes! Absolutely! Are you serious? This is the whole reason I went to culinary school. It will be an honor to fill that position for you."

Then Hattie turned her attention to Waylon and said, "Now, my dear boy, how do you feel about coming to work at the castle with your sister and being our grounds and maintenance man? There is far too much work that needs to be done for us to keep depending on outsiders. This old castle is made from brick, stone, and steel. I have been informed that you are an expert in those, are you not?"

Waylon, still light-headed over the family accepting his apology, answered Hattie with a quiet and shaky voice, "Yes, ma'am, I do all that well. I'm getting a better sense of what is right and wrong. I find it difficult to believe that all of you can forgive me. I even find it hard to believe God can forgive all the evil I have done! I'm going to counseling and church regularly, and I will be a faithful and dedicated employee. That I promise you!"

Hattie smiled, pleased by what she had heard. "Well, there's one slight correction on what you said. None of us here are employees. We are all family, working on the family estate. The employees on staff are very dear to us, so we are all one big happy family. Maribelle, Waylon, you are both genetically and spiritually part of our family. Therefore, you are working on your family's estate. God has given you both what you desired. A family, a purpose and a reason for being. God made it possible for you both to have a family who will love, protect, and stand by you. He has also given you both lucrative careers in the fields you enjoy. Isn't God amazing how He works all things out for our good?" The family agreed that only God could've set events up to end up the way they had. "Now as far as you feeling the heavy burden of regret for your past, read Psalm 51. Particularly verse 17. 'The sacrifices of God are a broken spirit: a broken and a contrite heart, O God, thou wilt not despise.'

"When our Father sees a sincere heart of repentance, He forgives and forgets! We must learn to forgive ourselves! David had sinned very badly! His heart was in misery over the vileness of his sin, so he went to God with a repentant heart. This chapter can help heal your concerns over forgiveness. And keep in mind, if God promises to forgive you, and we know God cannot lie, then for you not to forgive yourself is pure arrogance! You're saying your standards for forgiveness are higher than God's! Work on forgiving yourself and leave the forgiveness for your failures in God's hands!"

Jodi silently asked God to cause things to work out for the good of her elephant friends like he did for Maribelle and Waylon. Maribelle's suggestions were an amazing solution. Jodi's dad, Andrew, Sean, and her uncle Carl had a scheduled appointment with one of the judges the following week. It was their hope to get the necessary papers to purchase the elephants and transfer them to the Tennessee mountain. They already had the necessary documents from the governor of Tennessee and the chief of the mountain showing that all was arranged and ready for the elephants to arrive. Their argument of persuasion would be pointing out the large sum of money their county would be receiving instead of costing them the alternative of destroying the animals. Andrew planned to point out the fact that the state of Tennessee already had an elephant rescue habitat. Therefore, the governor of the state had no problem getting the necessary approvals for another one on the mountain. Adding a small herd of four elephants wasn't difficult, especially now that it was going to be funded and cared for by a generous donor!

*****

Andrew had negotiated with the judge, and they had agreed upon the price of three hundred and forty thousand dollars for all four of the elephants. Transferring them to the states would be an additional eleven thousand, so the judge could clearly see how it was in his town's best interest to sell the elephants rather than destroy them. The price might have been higher, but since the elephants were considered handicapped or high maintenance, the judge was more lenient on the price. The baby elephant was one of the high maintenance since it would require decades of feeding and vet bills. The matriarch, Mali, was already thirty years old and had begun needing more medical care. Libby had one of her legs broken by a stray poacher's bullet. It hit her leg and broke the bone. This was before little Toby was born. So Libby was rescued with the other members of her family. Her leg was set, and little Toby was born soon after her leg had healed. Pitiful Cuppy endured the worst of them all. Her tusks were removed down to her mouth. The poachers had been caught before they could do any more to her! If they had attempted to remove the tusks completely, Cuppy would have died. So the poachers sawed the tusks off as short as they could to save time! Tusks are rooted into the skull! The only way an elephant can lose their tusks completely and live is if the tusks fall out naturally on their own. It was a mercy that the knockout darts kept her from knowing what was happening to her. But she suffered a great deal when the infection set in. She almost lost her life!

All these complications brought the purchasing price down, and the pilot for the rescue zoo volunteered to deliver the elephants to their new mountain home for the price of the fuel for the trip. Since the family had a lawyer and a veterinarian taking full responsibility for the animals, it would relieve their zoo and their county of any responsibility for the violence the elephants may have shown. Plus, Sean had just been informed that the elephant's keeper, Evan, refused to press charges, claiming that he had stepped in front of the elephant's path, so they were not responsible for his injuries. When the legal process started, he felt pressure from the court to testify against his elephants, so he resigned his position, thinking he was going to lose his elephants anyway. When he heard that it was possible the elephants could be relocated to the Tennessee mountain, he asked the family if it would be possible for him to move with his elephants so he could continue to care for them. Evan informed them that he had no family ties to keep him in Ireland. The elephants were the only family he had.

Jodi was filled with such joy at the thought of Evan coming to the states to continue caring for the elephants! She hadn't even considered how leaving Evan would affect their lives! Of course, it would! They loved Evan, and he loved them. Jodi knew her dad could easily set things up for Evan to become a legal citizen of the United States, and she felt certain the chief and the mountain committee would allow the elephant's keeper to live near them.

Jodi said a silent prayer as the family continued talking over the best plan for all involved, "Father, You are amazing! Thank You for supplying a way to save the elephants. And You're making a way to bring their keeper with them. That's a detail that never even crossed my mind. But You knew what was needed, and You planned things perfectly as always. I love You, Father. You are so good to me!"

Little did Jodi know, but God had even more planned for her life and the lives of her family that she could have never guessed!

15

Jodi and the rest of the family sat restlessly waiting for the men to return, so they could hear the outcome of the judges ruling. Sean, Carl, and Andrew came back from the meeting with the judge in high spirits. Andrew informed them that the judge was persuaded to give leniency to the elephants because they would be leaving Ireland, and they had signed documents from the governor of Tennessee giving permission for the elephants to be transferred to his state. Plus, thanks to Maribelle, the hefty price he had asked for was easily paid in cash! Money, especially in that large amount, has a way of opening doors otherwise closed. Since the family would not be leaving Ireland for a few more weeks, the judge signed a petition allowing the elephants to stay at the zoo, and Evan could continue caring for them until the end of the year. However, since the zoo no longer owned the elephants, Andrew and his family would be required to pay a rental fee to the zoo for the habitat, and they would be responsible for food supplies for the elephants. Andrew signed the lease for the habitat rental and additional funds for the food necessary through to the end of the year. However, the family felt the new habitat would be finished in another week or so. It was their hope that the elephants could be moved before the end of the year. It all depended on how quickly the log cabin for Evan could be finished because the elephant's fence around the entire area and elephant house were almost complete. The contractors had all the able-bodied men and women residents on the mountain volunteering their labor to get the job completed in record time! Those who had no carpenter skills cooked around the clock so the others could keep the work going without the need to leave for food. Evan was thankful to have his elephants safe and so happy to be going with them.

Now that the zoo no longer owned the elephants and was not responsible for them, Jodi was once again allowed to visit them, and all seemed right with their world again. Of course, the plans were for Evan and the elephants to leave Ireland at the end of the week if everything went according to the plan in Tennessee.

Carl had been staying in touch with the contractor and was informed that Evan's house would be finished by then. The house plans Evan laid out for them was a simple bachelor's cabin. A three-room cabin was all he wanted. He had plenty of money for a bigger house, but he preferred smaller homes. He wanted it simple. The construction of such a simple house didn't take very long to complete.

Jodi was confident that her elephant friends would not have the chance to miss her because of all the new land they would have to explore when they first arrived. After a week or so later, she would be able to visit them again. That is until she had to return to Texas and school. Jodi knew she would be visiting Tennessee much more than her usual summer visit. With those elephants moving to the mountain, she planned to go there often!

Jodi was basking in the love that God shows his children. It was truly amazing how the money came about to make all those things possible. She wanted to have her aunt Hattie tell her what she thought about a particular Bible verse and all that had happened recently. Going down the eight flights of stairs to Hattie's bedroom, Jodi stood, once again, knocking at her great aunt's door.

Jodi sat on the sofa, seated at the foot of Hattie's bed, listening to the wise lady talk about Proverbs 13:22. "'A good man leaveth an inheritance to his children's children: and the wealth of the sinner is laid up for the just.' You know, Jodi, the Lord gives several examples of this verse. One very commonly known example is when the children of Israel were leaving Egypt. God told them to borrow from the Egyptians, and they accumulated enough things that when they left Egypt, they were very wealthy! I suppose you can assume that God was giving the Israelites a small payment for the services they had given to the Egyptians they were serving at the time. It was enough for them to start a new life in their new land. In Psalm 24, David tells us, 'The earth is the Lord's, and the fullness thereof; the world, and they that dwell therein.' When you understand that, there's no mystery as to why God does what He does. It is His to do with as He sees fit. Period. The money that came into Maribelle's life was gained from the mistakes of many. She has chosen to use it for the good of the ones who were extorted because of various reasons and to save the lives of four elephants. God knows what needs to be done, and He uses his people to do it. Even when the wicked don't know it, a lot of the time, they're part of God's plan too. The people on the list in that book who supposedly were involved or responsible for the murder, well, your dad had a meeting with our district attorney and those crimes are being investigated. Now it's getting late, so we need to go down with the rest of the family and have our devotions before I start dozing off to dreamland."

*****

Hattie sat in her favorite rocking chair and placed her reading glasses on to begin the family devotional. She was happy to see Maribelle and Waylon had stayed throughout the family discussions about the elephants and then decided to join their family devotions.

"Tonight, I thought it would be a good idea to go through a reminder of the important three steps for prayer. Maribelle and Waylon, this might help you in your young Christian lives to better understand the importance of prayer and how to pray. We sometimes are in a hurry and forget to be thankful or forget to ask God for forgiveness because we are so focused on asking for what we feel we need.

"There isn't a particular pattern or routine to follow because our prayers should come naturally from our hearts. Talking freely to our Father. However, when someone is new to praying, it's a good idea to have a guideline of reference to remember the important reasons why we pray.

"The first part of our prayers should be asking God for forgiveness. When you sit or kneel down to pray, ask Him to forgive you for all your unrighteousness. When a specific sin comes to your mind, ask God to forgive you for that sin and to remove it from your life and your mind. Pray for the strength to never repeat the sin again. Pray this daily, hourly if necessary, to keep your heart and mind clean before God your Father. The second step to prayer is Thanksgiving. Psalm 100:4 tells us we get into heaven's gates through thanksgiving. Be thankful unto Him and bless His name.

"Psalm 100:4, 'Enter into his gates with thanksgiving, and into his courts with praise: be thankful unto him, and bless his name.

"Everyone has something to be thankful for. If you are alive, you are breathing because God gave Adam his breath to breathe. You are breathing the very breath of God! That alone is reason enough to be thankful to him! Remember that old saying, 'Grace is when God gives us good things we don't deserve. Mercy is when he spares us the bad things we do deserve. Blessings are when he is generous with both!'

"We serve a wonderful and merciful and generous God who deserves our worship, our praise, and our eternal gratitude!

"The third step is warfare. We will always have things in our life that require a fight to win over the trials. When you open up the Bible and start reading, you have started an atomic bomb spiritually. When you read back to God the words that He said, you are fighting with weapons the enemy cannot fight against! If you feel confused and don't know what to pray for or what to say but your heart is heavy, be honest about how you feel. Tell God that. Jesus gave his disciples an example of how to pray in Matthew 6:9–13. 'After this manner therefore pray ye: Our Father which art in heaven, Hallowed be thy name. Thy kingdom come, thy will be done in earth, as it is in heaven. Give us this day our daily bread. And forgive us our debts, as we forgive our debtors. And lead us not into temptation, but deliver us from evil: For thine is the kingdom, and the power, and the glory, forever. Amen.'

"Just tell the Lord you are burdened and don't know what to say, then pray the example prayer Jesus gave us until the Holy Spirit intercedes for you and helps you know what to pray. There's a quote I read on the Internet one day that I've never forgotten. It's one of the things I'd love to hear God say to me when He first sees me. The quote said, "Pray so big and so often that when God meets you at heaven's gate, He says with a smile, 'Kid, you kept me busy.'" Now let's put these principles into the prayer for tonight.

"Father God, in the name of Jesus, I ask You to forgive me for all my sins. Cleanse me and renew a right spirit within me. If there are any sins in my life that I am not aware of or I am not remembering, anything in my life that displeases You or offends You, please bring them to my attention. When my time here on earth has finished, I want to hear You say, 'Well done, my faithful servant.' When my last prayer has been prayed, I will take comfort in knowing that my prayers helped in keeping the angels fighting the evil in this world. I thank You for the gift of this day and every day You bless me with. I thank You for the gift of a healthy body and mind. Simply having the ability to walk, talk, and see, those are blessings that not everyone has, and I want to thank You for all those blessings that I take for granted every day. Father, You have graciously supplied the help we needed for our bed and breakfast here at the castle. Not only have You supplied help, but You have also given us part of our family we didn't even know about. You are a loving and merciful God. Thank You for loving us. Now, Father, I have no need for anything tonight. You have already answered all the prayers I have laid before You up to this point. Thank You for your ever-present guidance and help. In Jesus' name, amen."

The family went to bed that night in awe of the way God had brought all the events together for the good of all his children involved.

16

Winter had set in full force in Ireland, and Christmas was just around the corner. The family was busy introducing Maribelle and Waylon as a part of the daily staff and informing them of their new responsibilities. Arrangements had been made to relocate the elephants at the end of the week. The mountain crew building the new habitat were informed to add a cabin for the elephant's keeper, Evan, on the grounds where his elephants would be living. The chief donated the three thousand acres so the elephants would never have to leave. The huge waterfall inside the elephant's habitat with fresh flowing water was a major asset, giving those large animals access to fresh flowing water year-round, plenty to bathe and play in during the hot summer months. The elephants would never feel caged again!

Jodi and her cousins continued their daily visits with the elephants while they were still there. The days had become cruelly cold, so they were forced to keep their visits inside the elephant house. Even still, they were required to stay bundled up with thick coats that made them resemble the cartoon Michelin Tire Man. The kids didn't seem to mind that at all. They knew their visits would soon come to an end because the elephants were going to a new and improved forever home. Since their visits were confined to the inside, Evan brought the bench from outside the habitat where Jodi sat to the indoors for the kids to sit on. All seemed right in their world again!

The aunts spent a great deal of time getting Maribelle and Waylon acclimated to their new surroundings and daily responsibilities. The two new family members seem to fit into the new surroundings easily. Having them added to the castle staff would free Sean and

Coleen to do more private investigative work. The aunts knew how much they enjoyed that and felt it was very important they had the freedom to work on the jobs that were so important to them. Just like the mountain investigation had been. Sean and Coleen had been faithful in helping their aunts with the bed and breakfast business since their parents died and left a void that needed to be filled. The aunts had depended heavily on their parents to run the business, so Sean and Coleen left the United States to fill in for their parents. They had done an excellent job and had seemed to enjoy it. But the aunts wanted to give them the freedom to follow their dreams to do what they had spent years in college learning to do. Now that Waylon and Maribelle had joined the staff, Sean and Coleen didn't need to feel obligated to spend every day at the castle holding down an everyday position.

Christmas was only a week away, and Coleen was due back home in the next few days. She had called to inform them that the wolves had passed their training with flying colors and had gone through all the drills with the same energy as when they were much younger. Coleen was very proud of them! She had asked to speak to Jodi.

"Hey, Coleen, we have all really missed you and the wolves! When will y'all be coming back home? Before we leave to go back home, I hope!"

"Oh yes! Definitely! Listen, Jodi, Sean has been keeping me informed on all that's happened while I've been away. Since the aunts have additional help at the castle, I was hoping, when I get back to the castle, you might enjoy going with me to do my Christmas shopping. I haven't found the time to do that, and now it's crunch time, and I must get it done. No more dillydallying around! I suppose you would say I've been a doofinhymer putting it off this long."

Jodi laughed. She was excited to spend some time shopping with her cousin Coleen. "That will be great fun! Just hurry home so we can get started!"

There were so many things to look forward to with the Christmas season just around the corner. Christmas was a holiday both the American and the Irish families celebrated every year, and it was an enormous treat to be celebrating it together this year!

Coleen was due to be home on December twenty-third, one day before they celebrated Christmas Eve. Christmas Eve night was when Jodi's family had always opened their gifts. Sean had called Coleen the day after she had talked with Jodi, asking her if she could invite the three boys to join them on the shopping trip. There was going to be a Christmas surprise for all the kids, and they all needed to be away from the castle to set it up! Coleen was totally on board with occupying the kids while the surprise was being set up. She told Sean to have Jodi invite the fellas to join them during their shopping because she had decided to take Shadow and Spirit with them. Taking the wolves to the shops around busy people was the best practice for all they were trained for. The obedience training was best tested in a chaotic situation. There isn't a better chaotic bunch of crowds than the Christmas shopping crowds! So it was all arranged to have a fun day out shopping with Coleen and the wolves on December twenty-third.

The whole town of Sea Cove loved Shadow and Spirit. They had watched them grow up from puppies to the confident law enforcers they were today! The citizens of Sea Cove knew if they saw Sean or Coleen, Shadow and Spirit would be with them. Each of the shop owners and businesses had *special* treats hidden away for when they were honored with a visit from Shadow and Spirit. It was quite evident that the wolves knew who had their treats and eagerly wanted to visit their shops! Animals are not typically allowed inside public businesses in Ireland. However, Shadow and Spirit were licensed agents of a highly respected investigative team; therefore, they were allowed access to any and all public places in Ireland! Those wolves were greatly respected and loved by the citizens of Sea Cove!

17

December twenty-third had *finally* arrived, and the kids had been instructed to meet up with Coleen and the wolves at the *Tis Tea Time Delicatessen* at twelve thirty sharp! Jodi had been up since before daybreak. Her excitement refused to allow her brain to sleep any longer. She quietly walked down the twelve flights of stairs on foot rather than taking the elevator, hoping the walking would help work out most of her pent-up excited jitters. Jodi walked into the library and found that Mansfield was already there. He was there starting the morning fire in the fireplace.

"Good morning, Miss Jodi. Looks like you're up with the chickens this fine winter morning. What could have possibly happened to cause a young girl like you to be up at the crack of dawn!"

Jodi giggled at Mansfield's joke about being up with the chickens. The aunts did have a small flock of chickens they kept for harvesting fresh eggs to keep the kitchen well stocked for all the grand meals, and she had heard the rooster's elaborately showy crows bright and early, but this morning, she woke up before the rooster. Jodi walked over to be near the blazing fire.

"I wasn't able to sleep any longer this morning. I'm too excited about seeing Coleen and the wolves again. Goodness, it's been over a month!"

"Ahh, yes. It will be jolly good, as ever, to have them back home again!" Mansfield could see how excited the young girl was, and he was also aware of the Christmas surprise she and her cousins would have, waiting for them Christmas Eve night.

*****

Coleen was waiting for her young cousins outside of the delicatessen. She knew the excitement of seeing them would cause Shadow and Spirit to be exuberantly happy, and that sort of energy would be frowned upon inside the tea house. No matter how much the owners loved the two wolves! Just as Coleen had predicted, the group was ecstatically happy! It was obvious to all who witnessed the reunion that Shadow and Spirit had missed the kids as much as the kids had missed them! In the middle of the happy greeting, Sean came to join them.

"I hope I'm not intruding. I thought it would be nice to join you all today."

The group was thrilled Sean wanted to join them. There had been a lot of stress in the past month, and the outing would be good for them all!

Going inside the little café, they found a curved booth close to the entrance glass door so Shadow and Spirit could easily see outside the door. The wolves laid on the floor, at the end of the booth. Sean was facing the front of the café with Shadow at his feet, facing the same way. Coleen was facing the wall with Spirit at her feet, facing Shadow. Their little group was eating and chatting. All was quiet and peaceful in the tea house. Shadow and Spirit actually napped while the family group was eating. During the groups catching up and enjoying their delicious food, two men dressed in long black overcoats walked into the café. Shadow and Spirit instantly became alert and on guard! That was very telling to Sean and Coleen because the wolves never reacted to people simply because they were strangers. Their training had taught them restraint and to be calm! Many customers had come through the doors while the wolves lay by the door, and not one *alert* stance had been made!

Sean was seated facing the cashier and watched as the men approached the counter. However, he wasn't able to see or hear what was being said or done. All appeared to be normal. The young cashier motioned for the woman who owned the Tis Tea House. She came to the register and opened it up. She withdrew the contents and handed it over to one of the men. The woman didn't make a scene, so everything looked to be business as usual. However, Shadow and Spirit felt something entirely different and had their senses working on overload! Sean put his hand down in front of Shadow's face. Coleen wasn't facing the front of the room and didn't understand why the wolves were reacting. Sean could see, but he didn't understand their reaction either. Seeing that Sean had told Shadow to lie quietly, Coleen did the same for Spirit. The two wolves silenced their low growling but never took their eyes off of the two men. Spirit had been lying, facing Shadow, but as soon as Coleen removed her hand from the front of Spirit's face, Spirit walked over and sat beside Shadow, facing the men in black. This deliberate move told Sean and Coleen that those men were up to no good! The wolves' attention was of such a fierce nature, it caused Sean and Coleen to pay attention! The situation was a bit unnerving because everything appeared to be normal. The two men turned to walk out of the café without ordering anything. They appeared to be leaving empty-handed. At least, that's the way it looked to anyone casually witnessing the activity in the little café.

As the men walked past Shadow and Spirit, the two wolves moved with the speed of a blink and stood blocking the exit! One of the men reached inside his coat. That was not a smart move. As soon as his hand went inside his coat, Shadow instantly had the man's arm in his mouth! A death grip inside his sharp, glistening white fangs! Spirit's attention was holding the other man at bay while Sean jumped to Shadow's side. Spirit had the other man's full attention and was holding him still as death! Her low, intensive growls, her ears laid back and fierce, her fur bristled! Her lips were curled up and back, and her perfectly cleaned fangs were on full display! The man could see Spirit's tongue pressed against her sharp fangs, in anticipation of a reason to bite! The terrified man spat out a whimper, and Spirit snarled and growled with a fierceness that caused the man to feel faint when he saw Spirit's back arch, ready for an attack! Shadow hung on to the other man's arm, despite all his loud screaming in pain! In the middle of the man's screams, Sean reached inside his overcoat to retrieve the gun hidden there and spotted a bulk of cash in the pocket as well.

"Well, now, what do we have here? Where do you suppose this bounty of treasure came from?" Sean motioned for Shadow to let the man's arm go. Shadow let go of his death grip but stayed alert to the man's every move! Both men stood there silent, not uttering a word.

Everyone in the little café were too stunned and fearful to move or utter a sound. They sat in their seats like frozen statues, watching in complete silence!

As soon as the wolves stopped the men and Sean had intervened, the owner of the café came up, standing behind the men. Sean asked her if she knew anything about the money in the man's pocket. The lady, visibly shaken, said the money belonged to the café.

"These men have just robbed my café of two thousand thirty-four pounds!"

Sean started calculating in his head. "That's approximately three thousand American dollars! Is that correct? It's still early in the afternoon!"

The lady smiled. "Yes, you're very close. We usually bring in around forty-five hundred pounds each day."

Sean acted surprised that such a small tea house would bring in close to six thousand dollars every day. "Sis, we're in the wrong business!" Sean was only teasing, trying to relieve some of the tension in the room. He knew the delicatessen had a successful online store, and their cakes and steaks were the best in the nation. "You men are not going to enjoy the holidays like you had planned. Thanks to our trusty companions here." Sean reached down and patted Shadow and Spirit on their heads as the Sea Cove guards were entering the café doors. The cashier had pushed the silent alarm as soon as the men turned their backs to her.

This situation was the perfect example of why Shadow and Spirit were welcome in all the businesses of Sea Cove! The café owner walked over to Shadow and Spirit and placed two heavily loaded plates in front of them. She had given each of them one of the café's prized twelve-pound beef steaks!

"Only the best for our heroes today! This steak has been crowned the world's best fillet at the International Steak Competitions. It is grass-fed Angus. The judges described it as a *picture-perfect fillet with flavor to back it up!*"

Sean laughed at the eager and happy faces of Shadow and Spirit. "And from the way these two are devouring it up, I'd say they agree!"

Everyone in the little café laughed and gave the wolves loud applause with whistles as they watched the wolves licking their now empty plates, getting every last bit of flavor. The kids sat at their booth, watching in stunned awe as the whole situation began to become real to their shocked senses! It had happened so quickly, and just as fast as it had started, it was over!

18

All four of Coleen's cousins pleaded with her not to get them Christmas presents that year. They had been so preoccupied with the crime on the mountain that past summer, not one of them had the chance to earn any money for gifts during their summer break. Jodi grabbed hold of Coleen's hand.

"Seriously, Coleen, just being here in your wonderful Ireland is all the gift we need!"

The boys all chimed in, "Absolutely!"

Coleen looked at her cousins. How grown-up they had become. The crime on their mountain had changed them. There was a seriousness that had not been there before. It saddened Coleen to see how serious they had become because of that horrible experience, yet she was equally proud of how mature and conscientious her young cousins were.

"Okay, I will only get each of you one small item to put in your stocking."

Just like in the United States, the darkness of night came quickly for Ireland in the month of December. The temperature had fallen to a low of thirty-nine degrees, and the sea breeze caused it to feel much colder! There had been a rare snowstorm after returning from the café, and the land around the castle looked like a white fairyland! The long-awaited Christmas Eve night had finally arrived. The American family was enjoying a very white Christmas and were thrilled to see the snow falling as they peered through the frosted, thick paneled windows of the castle. The family all gathered in the castle's great room for their Christmas devotion and to open their gifts. Christmas

Eve night was the time for opening gifts. Christmas Day was for the delicious family meal.

As the whole family gathered into the great room, a roaring fire burning in the massive fireplace, Jodi and her cousins sat on the floor with the wolves. The remaining family, including Waylon and Maribelle, sat in different places around the warm fireplace, all eagerly waiting to hear the Christmas story. Aunt Hattie got her well-worn Bible down from off the shelf, while Aunt Coreen brought a tray of beautifully decorated Christmas cookies, with large mugs of Cadbury hot chocolate she and Maribelle had made for all to enjoy. The Cadbury chocolate is Ireland's undisputed best chocolate. Jodi and her cousins looked forward to enjoying it each time they visited Ireland. Of course, they had Cadbury chocolate in the United States, but only the Ireland aunts had the special recipe for the Christmas hot chocolate! The aunts refused to share it with anyone but promised to leave it in their will for each family member. Aunt Hattie watched the happy faces of her young niece and nephews.

"Children, that includes you, Sean, and Coleen…" Aunt Hattie smiled with a wink that held a great secret. Sean and Coleen knew there was to be a surprise, but they had no idea what the surprise was.

Then Hattie began again, "Kids, moms, and dads, I feel that tonight's Christmas story should be done by a senior family member other than myself. So without further ado, would the other senior family member and all other family members, please come and join us?"

Everyone in the room looked toward the doorway of the great room. The whole massive room was filled with the intake of awe-struck breath as none other than the Texas family walked through the door! Johnny immediately ran to give his grandmother a huge affectionate hug! He had missed her and hadn't realized that deciding to stay in Ireland would mean spending his first Christmas away from his grandmother. It had made him feel sad, and now it was the best Christmas he could ever remember! Patrick, Etta, and Danny had flown back to spend Christmas with their Ireland family. The crises at the horse farm had subsided, and all was back to normal. Seth and Elizabeth decided not to return. They were expecting a very special foal for Christmas this year and wanted to be there when the little thing decided to arrive. Aunt Hattie walked over to where Patrick sat in an overstuffed club chair. She handed him her precious Bible. "Would you do us the honor of reading the Christmas story to us this year?"

"I would be happy to do that, Aunt Hattie." Patrick put on his reading glasses and found the passage of scripture while the others sat waiting to hear the familiar story they heard every year. "You realize believers in Christ have a far better time at Christmas than anyone in the world. Simply because we know the real reason Christmas is celebrated. In many, many homes tonight, the Christmas story being read starts out by saying, ''Twas the night before Christmas.' That story is about a man who flies in a sleigh and goes down a chimney. That part was always a bit strange to me. Welcoming a strange man into your home, in the dead of night, while you and your whole family are sleeping…but I digress. We, as Christians, know that isn't the real Christmas story. The story we are reading tonight is the real Christmas story! This is the beginning of how God chose to become a man so he could save us all and we could live with him one day! That's a far superior story! Not only because it's miraculous and far more magical than the other story, but because this story is *true!* Now let us begin…"

19

Luke 2

And it came to pass in those days, there went out a decree from Ceasar Agustus that all the world should be taxed.

(And this taxing was made when Cyrenius was governor of Syria.)

And all went to be taxed, every one into their own city.

And Joseph went up to Galilee, out of the city of Nazareth, into Judaea, unto the city of David, which is called Bethlehem; (because he was of the house and lineage of David:)

To be taxed with Mary his espoused wife, being great with child.

And so it was, that, while they were there, the days were accomplished that she should be delivered.

And she brought forth her firstborn son, and wrapped him in swaddling clothes, and laid him in a manger; because there was no room for them in the inn.

And there were in the same country shepherds abiding in the field, keeping watch over their flock by night.

And, lo, the angel of the Lord came upon them, and the glory of the Lord shone round about them: and they were sore afraid.

And the angel said unto them, Fear not: for, behold, I bring you good tidings of great joy, which shall be to all people.

For unto you is born this day in the city of David a Saviour, which is Christ the Lord.

And this shall be a sign unto you; ye shall find the babe wrapped in swaddling clothes, lying in a manger.

And suddenly there was with the angel a multitude of heavenly hosts praising God, and saying,

Glory to God in the highest, and on earth peace, and good will toward men.

And it came to pass, as the angels were gone away from them into heaven, the shepherds said to one another, Let us now go even unto Bethlehem, and see this thing which is come to pass, which the Lord hath made known to us.

And they came with haste, and found Mary, and the babe lying in a manger.

And when they had seen it, they made known abroad the saying which was told them concerning the child.

And all they that heard it wondered at those things which were told them by the shepherds.

But Mary kept all these things, and pondered them in her heart.

And the shepherds returned, glorifying and praising God for all the things that they had heard and seen, as it was told unto them.

And when eight days were accomplished for the circumcising of the child, his name was called Jesus, which was so named of the angel before he was conceived in the womb.

20

After the Christmas story had been read and the Christmas Eve dinner had been eaten, the family returned to the great room where the kids opened their gifts. When Aunt Hattie realized Jodi was interested in the history of the castle, she and Coreen promptly sent all the information to the Sea Cove printers and had a hard-back book made for her and her cousins in an emerald-green vegan leather, lined in bright metallic gold. The book was of exceptional quality and had over four hundred pages. Jodi squealed in delight as she flipped through the pages, noticing all the history the book revealed, then she ran over to give her great aunts a big hug of gratitude. Roman, Reggie, and Johnny did the same. Johnny had misty eyes as he thanked the generous ladies for including him.

"I want to thank you for including me in this amazing gift. I will cherish it as long as I live!"

Aunt Hattie returned their grateful hugs. "Children, this old castle is your home. As long as you live, you will have a home here in Ireland! Johnny, you are part of this family. That book is a reminder to you to come anytime you get the chance!"

Coleen walked over to the fireplace to get her and Sean's simple gift. "You guys insisted on a promise to not get gifts this year, and we promised to only get stocking stuffers. So Sean and I don't have a grand gift like our dear aunts just gave you, but we hope it will serve as a reminder of your Ireland home, almost as much as the history book."

The kids reached inside the stockings and drew out two snow globes. They were special to the city of Sea Cove. The specialty gift shops there had snow globes custom-made as souvenirs for the tourists of Ireland. One was a 3D sculpture of the castle. It was impeccably done in every diminutive detail! The other globe was of the large animal rescue zoo. It had a privacy fence and an entrance gate with the intricately carved elephants standing on each side. What an amazing reminder of their two favorite places in Ireland! Each snow globe played the same melody, "The Rose of Tralee." As Jodi turned the key under the bottom of the globe, snowflakes swirled around the glass globe, and the music started to play. Aunt Hattie, Aunt Coreen, Sean, and Coleen all started to sing the melancholic Irish song.

The pale moon was rising above the
green mountain
the sun was declining beneath the
blue sea
When I strayed with my love to the
pure crystal fountain
that stands in the beautiful vale of Tralee.
She was lovely and fair as the
rose of the summer
Yet 'twas not her beauty alone
that won me
Oh no! 'Twas the truth in her eyes
ever beaming
that made me love Mary,
the Rose of Tralee.
The cool shades of evening their
mantle were spreading
And Mary, all smiling, was listening to me

The moon through the valley her
pale shades were shedding
When I won the heart of the
Rose of Tralee
Though lovely and fair as the
rose of the summer

Yet 'twas not her beauty alone
that won me
Oh no! 'Twas the truth in her eyes
ever beaming
that made me love Mary,
the Rose of Tralee.

*****

As the aunts, Sean, and Coleen sang, others joined in. Jodi had to continue turning the key to the music globe because the song was much longer than the little globe had space for. It was great fun and laughter as the group waited for the music to be *re-cranked*.

Aunt Coreen commented to her sister, "Brings back memories of the old phonograph and gramophones, doesn't it, sis?"

The family enjoyed singing along to the melancholy Irish tune. When the song was finished, everyone felt it had been a wonderful Christmas. Johnny said it was the best Christmas he'd ever had. Etta went over to her grandson.

Hugging him, she said, "Well, I hope the gift Patrick, Danny, and I have for you will cause you to feel that way even more. The three of us have reached a decision that we hope you will agree to and be excited about. Danny has decided to take the governor of Tennessee's offer and become their state homicide commander and will need a place to live. I realize you haven't voiced any concerns about leaving the mountain and your Christian school to live in Texas, but I am fairly certain you can't be thrilled about leaving your school going into your senior year. So if you agree, we think it would be great if Danny moved into the cabin with you. That way, you wouldn't be alone, and he would have a home as well."

Johnny was smiling from ear to ear. "Oh wow, that would be great!" Then looking over at Danny, he said, "Are you sure you don't mind sharing the cabin with me?"

Danny roared with laughter. "Uh, I think maybe I should be the one asking you that question. It is, after all, *your* cabin! I feel fortunate to have been offered such a great place to stay."

Etta sighed with relief. "Well, okay then, that's settled. The chief of the mountain has already approved Danny becoming a full-time citizen on the mountain. He said everyone who had helped to clean up that horror on his mountain was welcome to live there! Johnny, you will be eighteen soon and will be starting college after your senior year. I fully understand you will be needing independence from your old granny, and I hope this will be an amazing start for you. Now your new granddad has something to offer you."

Patrick pulled out some legal-looking papers, looking quite serious and said, "Johnny, my boy, you are close to eighteen years old. That's a grown man, in my opinion, so if what I'm about to offer you isn't something you want, then you just say it right out, and that will be all that's ever said on the subject. Your grandmother and I had these papers made up, and all you have to do to make it legal is sign them with your name. We thought with your grandmother's name changing, you might like the opportunity to add our family name with yours. Make it a hyphenated name of Blyth-O'Connor." Johnny was so surprised he wasn't able to speak. Grandad Patrick saw Johnny's surprise and teased him a little, "We think it would look impressive on a business card. How do you feel about that?"

Johnny sat there stunned. He never considered that even a possibility. "Wow! That would be amazing! I would feel so proud to add your family's name to mine! Thank you so much!"

Johnny walked over to where his granddad Patrick was sitting, holding out the adoption legal papers waiting to be signed. Johnny took the papers, looking at them like a calf staring at a new gate. Patrick held out a pen for Johnny to use. Johnny signed the papers with his original name and then added the signature of his newly added name for the first time. He sighed with contentment. "Grandmother, we are part of an awesome family!"

Etta smiled happily. "Well, now your new uncle Carl has some news from the chief to share with you as well."

Johnny watched as his uncle Carl swallowed down the last bite of the Christmas cookie he had been eating. He was curious about what the chief of their mountain wanted to say to him. "Johnny, when I called LW and Autumn's home to speak with the chief, he had a lot of questions about all four of you kids."

Carl laughed. "Of course, it was all through LW's translating from the chief to me, but I got the full message. All of you kids made quite an impression on him! The way you used good common sense and made wise decisions during the whole crime on his mountain is something he said he would never forget. So this is what he proposes for each of you. Johnny, when he asked what you plan to do after graduation, I informed him that it was your plan to become an expert in the field of plant pathology and specialize in plant diseases caused by infectious organisms. Did I remember that correctly?" Johnny nodded yes, unable to speak. "When the chief heard that, he was really excited and hoped you would take over his job of keeping his mountain plant life healthy and thriving. He's getting too old to keep up all that's required, and the herbs and trees are very important to him. He is offering you full-time employment, at top pay, if you will continue his daily surveillance and care for the plant life on his mountain. His family has all lived on the herbs that the mountain supplies. His ancestors started the planting of special herbs, and the chief and his family have continued that tradition all these years! He has a Patton trademark for a natural fertilizer for keeping that grass and herbs green and healthy all year. LW said it has an impressive online sales record. They take care of that for the chief. The elephants are in their new habitat now, and the grass there is as green as it is in the middle of summer. The chief said he would leave the Patton for the fertilizer in your name in his will if you agree to be the caretaker for his mountain." Johnny sat dazed at such a great opportunity. "So what do you say? Does that sound like something you might be interested in doing as a career?"

"Absolutely! That is *exactly* what my dream job would be! Sign me up just as soon as I get that diploma in my hand! What an amazing Christmas present! And just so you know, Grandmother Etta, I will never feel the need for independence from you! You have always been very generous in giving me space and independence my whole life, even as a young boy. I would enjoy having you live with me forever!" Etta had tears of love and pride in her eyes as she gave Johnny an affectionate hug.

Carl then turned his attention to his son Reggie. "Son, the chief has asked me if you would be willing to stay on his mountain after you graduate college and become the mountain and surrounding town's holistic doctor. He has never been to a medical doctor. I know it's really hard to wrap your head around, but he has never trusted them. The herbalist in his family is getting older and can't handle the burden of helping people with prescribing the herbs they need. The mountain people have grown to depend on their help to stay off medication. He offers help anytime you may need it and promises to build you a holistic building to see clients and an addition added to keep all your herbal supplements safe and healthy if you can commit to at least five years of practice on his mountain after you get your degree. Is that something you would like to do?" Reggie and Johnny both were amazed at the generosity of the chief! "Johnny, would you be willing to work with me in helping me keep a healthy supply of herbs from the mountain?"

"Sure thing. Absolutely!"

"Dad, you can tell the chief I'd be honored to fill that position for him and thank him for the offer! Wow, the chief is being extremely generous to us!"

"Yes, he is, son. He's so grateful for how all of you kids showed the strength of character while dealing with the heinous crime on his mountain."

Jodi's dad, Andrew, spoke to Roman, "Young man, it's my understanding that you will start law school in a year or so. Right after graduation."

Roman's eyes shot wide open. "Yes, sir! Just as soon as they hand me that diploma!"

Andrew laughed, pleased with the enthusiasm he saw in his young nephew. "Well, then I'd like to offer you a position in my practice as soon as you reach that stage in your studies. After you get your law degree, if you want it, you can become a junior partner in my firm. How does that sound?" Roman sat there with his mouth gaping open but unable to speak.

His dad spoke up for him, "I think his silence is a resounding yes!"

Everyone laughed, and the laughter brought Roman to his senses. "Oh my gosh! Absolutely yes! Thank you so much, Uncle Andrew!"

The next one to get the surprise of their life was Jodi. Her mom was the one to tell her all about how her life was going to be blessed beyond her dreams!

"Jodi dear, you haven't been forgotten. I guess you could say we've saved the best for last. This was before the chief knew about Evan moving to stay with the elephants, but he feels this would be something important to you anyway. He wants to know if you could be available to keep check on the elephants because he knew, from the information we gave him, that they have bonded with you. Do you remember that land across the narrow dirt road you kids were walking down when you spotted the old shack?" Jodi sat listening to her mother, chewing on her fingernail in anticipation of what she was about to hear. She was only able to nod yes. She remembered. Jodi wasn't in the habit of chewing her nails. She wasn't thinking clearly and was obviously overcome by all the fascinating news so far! "Jodi, stop chewing your nails!"

Her mother laughed as Jodi snapped to reality, looked down at her finger, folded her hands together on her lap, and said, "Sorry, Mom."

Her mother continued, "Anyway, the chief has sold us ten acres of that land. Your dad has hired a contractor who is, at this moment, in the process of building our new mountain home! It will be finished by the time we leave Ireland. It is directly across from the elephant's new habitat! You can look out your bedroom window or sit on your balcony and watch the elephants, and they will be able to see you. You will be close enough to talk to them every day without leaving home! You will be able to come home from college like your cousins and not stay in a cramped dorm room. Merry Christmas, sweetie. You now have the elephant you wanted when you were a small child."

Jodi was crying tears of joy as she hugged her parents. This was an amazing answer to a dream she never thought to pray for!

Uncle Carl cleared his throat to gain control of his emotions, saying, "Now, little lady, I realize you have a few more years of school than your cousins, but I have an offer for your future if you want it. When you do start college, I'd like to offer you my clinic and any services you will need to ace your classes. Plus, after you have earned your veterinary degree, you can work as another doctor in my clinic, and when the time comes for me to retire, the clinic will be yours!"

Jodi was overcome with all the gifts offered to her! "Oh, Uncle Carl! That is far more than I could have ever hoped for! That would be such a huge honor! Thank you so much!"

The kids' minds were whirling with all the fantastic news and opportunities given to them for Christmas! Aunt Hattie and Coreen had an amazing gift for their new family members. Aunt Coreen went around the group, serving up more of the beautifully decorated Christmas cookies she and Maribelle had made, while Aunt Hattie shared the news, "Maribelle and Waylon, we haven't forgotten about you two. Sister and I have the center fourth floor of the castle, for our personal space. At our age, we don't need or want any more than that. Sean and Coleen have the north wing. Pastor John has a section of the east wing because that is the closest to the chapel and where the majority of the guests prefer because of the views from that side of the castle. Pastor John thought it would be best if he was closer to where the guests would be in case anyone needed him for anything, he would be easier to find. Sean, Coleen, sister, and I would like to offer you two parts of the west wing of the castle for your home. That whole wing is on the main level of the castle, making it easier for each of you to go where you need to go every day. You can decorate it however you please. There are six bedrooms, four bathrooms, two large living rooms, and a small kitchen with a pantry and utility. This will be your personal space. Of course, the whole castle will be your home. Just consider that part your very own. You can even have a locksmith change the door handles with locks if you would like. I would recommend that, by the way."

Aunt Hattie laughed. "We have a lot of guests that love to look around while they're here. You will be working here every day now, so it only makes sense that you live here too. The whole area is large enough that you should never feel the need to leave. And should either or both of you decide to marry and have a family, there is more space in that wing that could be added if needed. How does that sound to you?"

Maribelle and Waylon were overwhelmed by the generosity of their new family! Never had they ever known such genuine kindness or acceptance!

Maribelle spoke for them both, "We would be thrilled to live in such a beautiful place and call it home! We are humbled by your kindness and feel blessed to be part of your family! Thank you so much!"

The kids' minds were whirling with all the fantastic news and opportunities given to them for Christmas! Aunt Hattie opened her Bible to read.

"Kids, this is the perfect example of Matthew 6:8 where we are told that the Father knows what we need before we even ask Him! 'And it shall come to pass, that before they call, I will answer; while they are yet speaking, I will hear. You children have been given answers to prayers you never prayed but your Father knew what would make your lives sweeter.' Like it says in James 1:17, 'Every good gift and every perfect gift is from above, and cometh down from the Father of lights, with whom is no variableness, neither shadow of turning.'"

21

Hattie looked at her family, all beaming with joy. "God our Father in heaven delights in giving good gifts to His children. The greatest gift He has given us is the Holy Spirit. Continue to have faith in God. Talk with Him often!"

Patrick agreed, "Absolutely! Aunt Hattie is right. Only by listening to the Holy Spirit will any of us have a successful life. Kids, we've been calling back and forth with your aunts, setting up a time for us to return for this Christmas surprise, and they have kept us informed on all that has happened since we left Ireland. I now know why Aunt Hattie was led to read those verses in the book of Luke and John earlier after Maribelle came to stay. If you look back on all the events that have taken place this year, those verses make perfect sense! First, there was that awful cruel attempt to start a canned hunt on the beautiful Bear Mountain in Tennessee then the horrible injection of snake venom in innocent Maribelle's ankle. Next was the unthinkable attempt to kidnap Jodi, and only God knows what that crazy man's plans were should he have succeeded! Then as if that wasn't enough, there was the attempted robbery at the tea house down the road from here. What do all these have in common? Greed! The love of money! Those verses Aunt Hattie read to us tell us how God wants us to think of money! Something came to my mind while we were singing "The Rose of Tralee." It's a really sad story, and it is tragic because of money. A nineteenth-century wealthy merchant named William fell in love with Mary O'Connor. Isn't that fascinating? She had the same last name as my family. It was love at first sight, but they were not permitted to marry because Mary was a maid—the

133

differences in social class between the two families. William was very upset and decided to travel for a while. A year later when he returned to Tralee, he discovered that Mary had died. He was brokenhearted and expressed his love for her in the song "The Rose of Tralee." So you see, children, here again is another proof that what the Bible says about money is true: "For the love of money is the root of all evil: which while some coveted after, they have erred from the faith, and pierced themselves through with many sorrows" (1 Timothy 6:10).

"Kids, if you will grow up depending on God for all your needs, you will have a successful life! Keep those verses Aunt Hattie read to us at the beginning of our visit here. Meditate on them. Make them a real part of your daily lives, and you will never have a wrong outlook on money. Here are a couple of examples in the Bible. In Mark chapter 10, we read of a man who was very moral. He felt he had kept all the commandments, but Jesus let him know he was lacking in an area of his life. His love for money was keeping him from God. Let's read that.

"Mark 10:17–31, 'And when he had gone forth into the way, there came one running, and kneeled to him. And asked him, Good Master, what shall I do that I may inherit eternal life?

"And Jesus said unto him, why callest me good? There is none good but one, that is, God. Thou knowest the commandments, Do not commit adultery, do not kill, do not steal, do not bear false witness, defraud not, honour thy father and thy mother.

"And he answered and said unto him, Master, all these have I observed from my youth.

"Then Jesus beholding him loved him, and said unto him, One thing thou lackest: go thy way, sell whatsoever thou hast, and give to the poor, and thou shalt have treasure in heaven: and come, take up the cross and follow me.

"And he was sad at that saying, and went away grieved: for he had great possessions. And Jesus looked round about, and saith unto his disciples, How hardly shall they that have riches enter into the kingdom of God.

"It is easier for a camel to go through the eye of a needle, than for a rich man to enter into the kingdom of God.

"And they were astonished out of measure, saying among themselves, Who then can be saved?

"And Jesus looking upon them saith, With men, it is impossible, but not with God: for with God all things are possible.'

"Jesus knew the man had an unhealthy love and dependence on money and was offering him the opportunity to break free from the hold it had on his life. That man, even though he was a very moral man, died without Christ because of his love for money.

"The *eye of the needle* this verse is talking about is not an actual needle one would sew with. It was a gateway into the city of Jerusalem. It was so narrow that heavily loaded riders would have to unload their camels before they could pass through it. It was Jesus' way of saying that the young man needed to unload the heavy hold his riches had on his life before his heart could accept Christ.

"We as Christians have many opportunities in our lives to be an example of Christ to others, but many times, we overlook them as insignificant. Oftentimes, many think they are too young to make a difference. Let's take a look at a young boy who went to hear Jesus teach and was offered an opportunity to help by sharing his lunch.

"Luke 9:12–17, 'And when the day began to wear away, then came the twelve, and said unto him, Send the multitude away, that they may go into the towns and country round about, and lodge, and get victuals: for we are here in a desert place.

"But he said unto them, Give ye them to eat. And they said, we have no more than five loaves and two fishes; except we should go and buy meat for all this people.

"For they were about five thousand men. And he said to his disciples, Make them sit down by fifties in a company.

"And they did so, and made them all sit down.

"Then he took the five loaves and two fishes, and looking up to heaven, he blessed them, and brake, and gave to the disciples to set before the multitude.

"And they did eat, and were all filled: and there were taken up fragments that remained to them twelve baskets.'

"John 6:9 lets us know it was a young boy's lunch that was used. 'There is a lad here, which hath five barley loaves and two small fishes: but what are they among so many?'

"Now he was only a young boy, but since he was obviously old enough to go on his own to go hear Jesus teach, we can assume he was old enough to realize his small lunch would not feed all that was there. Logic would tell him to keep his food for himself. Why should he go hungry just because the others didn't have the forethought to bring their own food? That fact did not stop the boy from willingly giving up all he had in an effort to help. Can you see the difference in the attitude of this young boy and the rich young man? Because the young boy was willing to give what he had, he witnessed a miracle that day. A miracle that came about because of his willingness to give! He saw his tiny, insignificant lunch feed a multitude of people. The story doesn't end there, not by a long shot! That boy took home twelve baskets of food for his family! One preacher jokingly described it as the boy took home enough food to start a small delicatessen! That is how God works! You can't out-give God!

"II Corinthians 9:6–11 says this, 'But this I say, He which soweth sparingly shall reap sparingly; and he which soweth bountifully shall reap bountifully.

"Every man according as he purposeth in his heart, so let him give; not grudgingly, or of necessity: for God loves a cheerful giver.

"And God is able to make all grace abound toward you; that ye, always having all sufficiency in all things, may abound in every good work. As it is written, he that dispersed abroad; he hath given to the poor: his righteousness remaineth forever.

"Now he that ministereth seed to the sower both minister bread for your food, and multiply your seed sown, and increase the fruits of your righteousness;

"Being enriched in every thing to all bountifulness, which causeth through us thanksgiving to God.'

"If we give generously to others, from a sincere heart, God will generously provide for us. God loves us more than we can ever love ourselves. Think about that for a moment! Now why wouldn't you trust an all-wise, an all-knowing, all-powerful God with your finances, with your life? God can do more than we could ever ask, think, hope or dream! Have faith in God. Talk with him often!

"Mark 11:22–26 tells us, 'Have faith in God. For verily I say unto you, That whosoever shall say unto this mountain, be thou removed and be thou cast into the sea; and shall not doubt in his heart, but shall believe that those things which he saith shall come to pass; he shall have whatsoever he saith. Therefore, I say unto you, what things so ever you desire, when you pray, believe that ye receive them, and ye shall have them. And when ye stand praying, forgive, if ye have ought against any: that your Father also which is in heaven forgive your trespasses. But if ye do not forgive, neither will your Father, which is in heaven, forgive your trespasses.'

"Kids, this is a promise from God! All you have to do to receive this promise is to believe it! The God we serve is amazing, and He has adopted us into his family through His Son Jesus, and He allows us to call Him Father…Abba Father! The same way I adopted Johnny into my family by giving him my name, God, the Father, has adopted us through His Son and made us part of His family. God has many names, and each one is extremely important, but Abba Father is an Aramaic word that expresses affection, trust, and confidence. It shows how close and intimate God wishes to be with us. What an amazing privilege that God himself encourages us to call him Abba Father! Kids, don't ever neglect such an amazing grace of God's love toward us!"

22

The winter days were in full force. Gone were the mild chilly winds, replaced with the harsh cold, freezing air! The kids were forced to spend most of their time inside the castle. There were lots of things to see and do in that grand old place, but Jodi missed her visits with Toby. Having Shadow and Spirit back was a great help. She had missed spending time with them too. Jodi knew the elephants were too busy exploring their new home to think about her. They were in a heaven on earth, and the weather there would rarely get to freezing. They would have fresh, flowing water year-round and a beautiful waterfall to play in. Thanks to the intelligent chief, they had green grass to eat, play, and sleep on. She had been there every summer for most of her life. Now she would be living there too. What an amazing life God had planned out for her! Only one more week in Ireland then she and her family would be going home. Home to Tennessee!

Jodi's uncle Danny would be living there now too. What a big change in everyone's life. She would have never even dreamed her life could change so much in one year's time! Jodi sat in the castle's library. Now that she was forced to stay inside, she had spent the last few days looking through the antique books in the castle's library, books that had been collected for hundreds of years! She could finally understand her cousin's fascination with the books. One could spend a lifetime reading all the new information from those ancient books and never get bored, information that is no longer practiced or even heard of!

Jodi sat in the beautiful library, flipping through some of the antique art books. The young girl was fascinated by how art had changed over the centuries since she was born. There were so many varieties of art. So many styles. The Mona Lisa, The Last Supper, The Starry Night, Girl with a Pearl Earring…she was intrigued by the talents of artists. Paintings, sculpture, photography, the world seemed endless at the possibilities of art forms! Jodi stopped on the information about the Mona Lisa painting. Such a simple picture of a lady, with the pose of someone having their photograph taken. This painting had been talked about for centuries! Painted by Leonardo Da Vinci, 1503–1506. Jodi read some of the fun facts about the famous painting and was surprised to discover it had been stolen in 1911, and the thief made the painting famous when the newspapers spread the story of the crime. After it was returned, it was celebrated as a masterpiece.

Jodi made her way to the sitting room, where the family gathered each night for their family devotions. Her mind was thinking about the things Granddad Patrick talked about the night before, how greed had been the common thread joining all the crimes that year. It seemed to her that it had been a problem since the beginning of time. All the family was already there, getting ready for the devotional, when Jodi entered the room.

"I've just read the most interesting things about the famous Mona Lisa painting. Did y'all know it was made famous because it was stolen and that brought a lot of attention to it?"

Her uncle Danny smiled. "No kidding…well, I have something along those lines you might find interesting. It goes along with what you just shared and what dad shared with us last night."

The room was still, each person thinking about the Bible verses and examples they had heard from Patrick's teaching of how Christians should think about money. Danny was a bit more serious and reflective as he continued, "Dad, I have a story to add to all you said last night. I have just finished with a case that fits everything you were talking about, and now little Jodi just reminded me of it again. There was a major crime going on in Texas just before the crime on the Tennessee mountain. The criminal had stopped, giving me the freedom to help with the Tennessee crime, then out of the blue, for no apparent reason, it started again! When we left Ireland last month, our team at the station found out the criminal resumed the same as before. These criminals went into homes and stole their very valuable oil and pastel art. Our investigative team was completely baffled as to how the criminal was doing it. Usually, expensive art is stolen for the ransom because it is too difficult to sell it without getting caught. But this thief always left a replica behind! The replicas were done by a master art plagiarist! The art pieces left behind were identical in every detail except for the oils and chalks used to do them. To the naked eye, the colors, the technique, and everything else were spot on! It took an independent art expert to determine the mediums used in the paintings were modern paint and chalks and not the older pigments the antique paintings were made with.

"I wasn't aware of this before, but today's global art market is a billion-dollar business! Since the thief was leaving replicas behind, we felt certain they didn't want a ransom for its return. They obviously already had a buyer waiting for the painting. Anyway, one of the owners of the art pieces had what they thought was their art reappraised for their insurance. Only to find out what they had wasn't their original art! That alerted others in their neighborhood to have their paintings reappraised, and that's how they all discovered their paintings had been stolen and replaced with forgeries!

"It has taken our team over a year, but the criminal is now behind bars. Correction, criminals. Turns out, the art thief is none other than a mother and her five sons!" The room was filled with loud gasps! Danny held up his hands. "Wait, wait! It gets even more shocking! If you start such large gasps now, you'll surely hyperventilate before you hear it all!" Everyone laughed out loud but waited with bated breath to hear the rest of the shocking story. Danny took a deep breath and continued, "The thief was the mother. She is a former gymnast who has won gold medals in artistic, rhythmic, power tumbling, and acrobatic gymnastics! This woman had all the tools and experience needed to sail over balconies, scale the rooftops, and climb two- and three-story buildings. And the most difficult part to believe is, she did all this at the age of seventy-three!"

The room was filled with exclaims of shocked surprise. Shadow and Spirit let out alerted barks because of the sounds from the people in the room. The gasps of shock caused the wolves to think of possible danger. Coleen ran over to them and started calming them, reassuring them that all was fine. No reason to be on guard. Maribelle left the room and came back, bringing mugs of the Christmas hot chocolate. She felt honored to be given a permanent position at the bed and breakfast, a residence in the castle and an honored place in the family. She wanted them to see that she was thankful and intended to take all those blessings seriously!

Sean took a big swallow of the hot chocolate and then chewed on a softened marshmallow, asking Danny, "How is it possible for a seventy-three-year-old woman to do a crime like this all on her own? How did she manage to get rid of those paintings? Did she do the forgeries herself too? Didn't you say she has five sons? Where do they come into this?"

Danny sat, sipping on his hot chocolate, saying, "Patience, I'll tell y'all everything. Just hold your taters!" He laughed at Sean's interest. He knew Sean had a great interest in investigating too.

Then everyone roared with laughter when they heard Maribelle ask Coreen, "What are taters?"

Aunt Coreen answered her question in Gaelic, "Tatairs, prátá. It's southern slang for potatoes. It means hold your horses or wait a minute."

Maribell laughed. "Oh, I see. Very well. Please continue with your story, Danny."

"Well, that's where her sons come into the picture. Three of them distributed the paintings to the buyers all over the world to different wealthy collectors. One of the sons was the master forger. The other was the family accountant. You would think that a family with that much talent could think of a better way to use those talents. They had been stealing art for over a year. Doing the art crimes had made them millions of dollars. They had stolen art from ten different homes. There's usually only a ten-year prison sentence for art theft, so with good behavior and considering her advanced age, it's highly possible this woman would outlive her sentence. Her sons may not be as fortunate. In the last attempt to steal a painting, the woman came sailing through a balcony window she had left open for her quick entrance and fast getaway. She came to steal the painting in the middle of the night. The woman of the house had gotten up and was going downstairs when the thief came flying through the window, and the thief accidentally knocked the woman over the balcony, down three stories. The woman of the house was killed instantly! Now this very talented seventy-three-year-old woman will spend the rest of her life in prison. The life she led and introduced to her sons has caused them to spend their lives in prison as well! The actions of this seventy-three-year-old woman have cost her and her sons their freedom and taken the life of a young woman! All because of greed! I told that story to say here is another example of the trouble people go to for money!"

Patrick started flipping through his Bible. "Perfect example, son. All the more reason, we as Christians need to make it a daily practice to live by faith. Let God take care of our needs. Faith does not live by things we can see, appearances, not even by explanations. Just because we don't understand what God is doing doesn't mean we're to stop living by faith! Faith lives by God's promises! No matter what our circumstances, God expects us to trust him for our needs. Habakkuk 3:17–18 says, 'Although the fig tree shall not blossom, neither shall the fruit be in the vines; the labour of the olive shall fail, the fields shall yield no meat; the flock shall be cut off from the fold and there shall be no herds in the stalls...'" Patrick paused to look at his family. "Things sound really bad here, doesn't it? Let's see how Habakkuk said he would respond if things got that bad. 'Yet I will rejoice in the Lord. I will joy in the God of my salvation. The Lord is my strength and he will make my feet like hind's feet, and he will make me walk upon mine high places.'

"This is proof that no matter how dreary things may get in our lives, God wants us to trust Him. We need to realize that He knows how to take care of us no matter how bad things get down here. The prophet Habakkuk asked God a lot of hard questions about things. God answered Habakkuk by letting Him know He is God. He had a plan! Even though Habakkuk was confused and sad about things, God assured him that He, Himself, was going to watch over them. Habakkuk trusted that God had a reason for allowing those things to happen around him. We can trust that God's ways and reasons are far better than ours will ever be! Always remember, no matter how bad the circumstances, Psalm 48:1 tells us, 'Great is the Lord, and greatly to be praised in the city of our God, in the mountain of his holiness!' Remove the spirit of lack from your hearts and minds. God enjoys supplying our needs. Remember the poor widow who had sons and a large debt? Let's read about her in II Kings 4:1–7.

"'Now there cried a certain woman of the wives of the sons of the prophet unto Elisha saying, Thy servant my husband is dead; and thou knowest that thy servant did fear the Lord: and the creditor is come to take unto him my two sons to be bondmen. And Elisha said unto her, what shall I do for thee? Tell me, what hast thou in the house? And she said, Thine handmaid hath not anything in the house, save a pot of oil. Then he said, Go, borrow thee vessels abroad of all thy neighbors, even empty vessels; borrow not a few. And when thou art come in, thou shalt close the door upon thee and upon thy sons, and shalt pour out into all those vessels and thou shalt set aside all that which is full. So she went from him, and shut the door upon her and her sons, who brought the vessels to her; and she poured out. And it came to pass, when the vessels were full, that she said unto her son, Bring me yet a vessel. And he said unto her, There is not a vessel more. And the oil stayed. Then she came and told the man of God. And he said, Go, sell the oil, and pay thy debt, and live thou and thy children of the rest.'

"The widow woman's son was going to be sold as slaves to work off the family debt. God's servant Elisha told her how to save her family, and she obeyed him. She had more than was needed to fill all the pots they had borrowed. Oil, usually olive oil, was a precious item in the international trade. There was plenty to sell to pay the debt and more left over for the family to live on. God will provide for his children if we will only trust and obey. Remember the words to the old hymn, trust and obey? Those words are very true!

> When we walk with the Lord in the light of His
> word,
> what a glory He sheds on our way!

While we do His good will,
He abides with us still and with all who will trust
    and obey.
Trust and obey,
for there's no other way to be happy in Jesus but
    to trust and obey!

Jodi sat listening to all she had heard about how much God wants His children to trust Him. She was very thankful to have God in her life! He had been her source of peace throughout her life. She had many examples of where He had answered her when she prayed and examples of where He had helped her or given her blessings she never thought to ask Him for. The most perfect example of that was the elephants in her life. She was very thankful she had given her life to Christ. She had so many blessings she couldn't count them all. Now in the next few days, she would be leaving Ireland and going to her new home in Tennessee, where she would see her elephants every day! There was no reason anyone would ever need to be greedy or money hungry if they would only trust in God. Hebrew 13:5–8 came to Jodi's mind.

> Let your conversation be without covetousness; and be content with such things as you have: for he hath said, I will never leave thee, nor forsake thee. Jesus Christ is the same yesterday, and today and forever.

Yes, God was always the same. He never changes. He is the only true God! Jodi was reminded once again of what her grandad Patrick always said, "God is good, and His mercies endure forever!"

Author's Note

When we sin, our guilt is ever before us—demanding that we acknowledge what we have done wrong! Sometimes, that guilt makes us feel God could never forgive us, even after we have confessed and asked for forgiveness, just like Waylon felt after asking the family and God to forgive him. Aunt Hattie instructed him to read this chapter. King David had sinned and felt the weight of that sin. This is his prayer to his Father. Let his prayer encourage you to have faith in God's amazing mercy to those who come to him with a broken heart, asking Him for forgiveness.

Psalm 51

> Have mercy upon me, O God, according to thy lovingkindness: according unto the multitude of thy tender mercies blot out my transgressions.

> Wash me thoroughly from mine iniquity, and cleanse me from my sin.

> For I acknowledge my transgressions: and my sin is ever before me.

> Against thee, thee only, have I sinned, and done this evil in thy sight: that thou mightiest be justified when thou speakest, and be clear when thou judgest.

Behold, I was shapen in iniquity; and in sin did my mother conceive me.

Behold, thou desirest truth in the inward part: and in the hidden part thou shalt make me know wisdom.

Purge me with hissop, and I shall be clean: wash me, and I shall be whiter than snow.

Make me hear joy and gladness; that the bones which thou hast broken may rejoice.

Hide thy face from my sins, and blot out all mine iniquities.

Create in me a clean heart, O God; and renew a right spirit within me.

Cast me not away from thy presence; and take not thy Holy Spirit from me.

Restore unto me the joy of my salvation; and uphold me with thy free spirit.

Then will I teach transgressors thy ways; and sinners shall be converted unto thee.

Deliver me from bloodguiltiness, O God, thou God of my salvation: and my tongue shall sing aloud of thy righteousness.

O Lord, open thou my lips; and my mouth shall shew forth thy praise.

For thy desirest not sacrifice; else would I give it: thou delightest not in burnt offering.

The sacrifices of God are a broken spirit: a broken and contrite heart, O God, thou wilt not despise.

Do good in thy good pleasure unto Zion: build thou walls of Jerusalem.

Then shalt thou be pleased with the sacrifice of righteousness, with burnt offering and whole burnt offering: then shall they offer bullocks upon thine altar.

In the fourteenth verse, David mentions his sin of bloodthirstiness. If that is not the sin you are coming before God with, you can easily pray this prayer and tell God what you are repentant of. In our days of grace, God no longer accepts the same type of sacrifices of King David's day. God requires us to come to Him with a broken heart and accept Him as Lord and Savior of our life! Our bodies are the sacrifice He now requires. We are to live our lives believing in Him, through faith, to please Him!

Romans Road to Salvation

All have sinned and fall short of the glory of God. (Romans 3:23)

God shows His love for us in that while we were still sinners, Christ died for us. (Romans 5:8)

The wages of sin is death, but the free gift of God is eternal life in Christ Jesus our Lord. (Romans 6:23)

If you confess with your mouth that Jesus is Lord and believe in your heart that God raised him from the dead, you will be saved. (Romans 10:9)

Everyone who calls on the name of the Lord will be saved. (Romans 10:13)

Sinner's Prayer for Salvation

The words alone will not save you. You must sincerely believe in what you are praying.

> Heavenly Father, I come to you asking You to forgive my sins. I confess with my mouth and believe in my heart that Jesus is Your Son, and He died on the cross at Calvary that I might be forgiven and have eternal life in the kingdom of heaven. Dear God, I believe that Jesus rose from the dead. I ask You to forgive me of all my sins, and I ask You to come into my life and be my Lord and Savior. And I will worship You all the days of my life. Because your Word is truth, I confess with my mouth that I am born again and cleansed by the blood of Jesus! In Jesus' name, amen.

About the Author

Reba Whitley has served in church ministries, with her husband, for over thirty years. She is the author of The Mountain Shack Mystery. She enjoys writing stories that encourage people to have a close relationship with God. It is Reba's prayer that her stories inspire people to keep their faith in God strong and to talk with Him often!